"This workbook is an invaluable resource for anyone struggling with significant shame or self-criticism. Whether used on its own or in conjunction with therapy, this workbook guides the reader through practical and enlightening exercises and tools designed to cultivate self-kindness. More than just a science-based guide, this workbook serves as a supportive companion for anyone who finds themselves in a battle with their inner self-critic."

—**Jenna LeJeune, PhD,** licensed psychologist; president of Portland Psychotherapy Clinic, Research, and Training Center; and coauthor of *Values in Therapy*

"A harsh inner critic can cripple our efforts to build the life we want to have, and this book can help. In this clear, insightful, and intensely useful book, Shawn and Holly help us explore where those harsh voices in our heads come from, and teach us how to replace them with a helpful, compassionate inner voice."

—**Russell Kolts, PhD,** professor of psychology at Eastern Washington University, and author of *CFT Made Simple* and *The Anger Workbook*

"I've been waiting for a workbook like this, and it delivers big time! It offers a deep exploration into the roots of self-criticism, helping clients make sense of their inner critic, then provides a step-by-step approach for building self-compassion. Packed with engaging exercises and practical tools, it's the perfect companion for therapists and clients alike, ensuring they have everything they need for real, lasting change."

—**Brian Pilecki, PhD,** clinical psychologist, psychedelic researcher, and author of *ACT-Informed Exposure for Anxiety*

"*You are your worst critic* is an all-too-common refrain of our shared human experience. With *The Inner Critic Workbook*, Shawn and Holly reveal from their deeply shared wisdom: a sure pathway to transform that inner pain into transformative growth. By putting these principles into practice, you are in the safe hands of two authors with deep professional insight who have done this work through passionately lived experience."

—**Grant Dewar, PhD,** life educator, and author of *The Self-Forgiveness Workbook*

"Get ready to deeply understand yourself and your inner thoughts—both the helpful and the hurtful. This beautiful workbook is informative, encouraging, and transformational. If you do the work, you will be changed. I highly recommend you give it a shot!"

—**Jill Stoddard, PhD,** author of *Imposter No More, Be Mighty,* and
The Big Book of ACT Metaphors

"Shawn and Holly have written a beautiful, personal, and useful guide to softening the critical inner voice that strips vitality from life, and finding a path toward thriving that involves tenderness and gentleness toward yourself. If you find yourself not feeling like you measure up, not quite good enough, or afraid to give yourself the same tenderness and gentlehearted warmth you give others, this book is for you."

—**Matthew D. Skinta, PhD, ABPP,** associate professor of psychology at
Roosevelt University, and author of *Contextual Behavior Therapy for Sexual
and Gender Minority Clients*

"If you're hard on yourself, this workbook is a gift. *The Inner Critic Workbook* is both compassionate and deeply practical, helping you develop a kinder relationship with yourself through engaging, science-backed exercises. Highly recommended for anyone who struggles with self-criticism."

—**Jason Luoma, PhD,** scientist studying shame and compassion, CEO of
Portland Psychotherapy, and author of *Learning ACT* and *Values in Therapy*

The
Inner Critic
Workbook

Self-Compassion and Mindfulness Skills to

Reduce Feelings of Shame,

Build Self-Worth, and Improve Your

Life and Relationships

SHAWN COSTELLO WHOOLEY, PsyD
HOLLY YATES, LCMHC

New Harbinger Publications, Inc.

Printed in the United States of America

27   26   25

10   9   8   7   6   5   4   3   2   1   First Printing

This book is dedicated to the beautiful spirit of Leann Harris. Her no-nonsense invitation to "just write the book already" was the nudge we needed. Dear Leann, your voice is in our heads, still, and your beautiful soul lives in our hearts. Thank you.

Contents

Acknowledgments

We offer our deepest appreciation together.

For each other. We realized while writing this workbook together that although our approaches are different, our voices are the same. We are each other's teacher. Compassion and love for one another triumphs over the most painful inner narratives. Love you! We bought a zoo!

For our families, Brian, Danny, Bill, Liam, Collin, and Riley. Your unwavering faith in our ability to write has not gone unnoticed. You have given your unconditional support, and for that, we are grateful beyond measure.

For our teachers and mentors, Mavis Tsai and Sonja Batten, your guidance and friendship has been immeasurable.

For our editorial team, Jess O'Brien and Vicraj Gill, for your patient guidance; Matt McKay, who came to our workshop, liked what he heard, and invited us to write this book; and Marisa Solis, whose handholding was the cherry on top.

For our clients, many of whom contributed to this book through countless sessions of tears and reflection. Walking side by side, you helped us figure out this work of quieting the Inner Critic. Special thanks to Claire, Kay, Melissa, and Alex, for your willingness to serve as foundations for our composite case examples.

And for our chosen family, you know who you are, without whom, truly, this book would not be. Your unconditional, unquestionable support and love has sustained us in small ways and big. You have been the model of compassion and loving discipline. You help us bring compassion to our own Inner Critics, every day. So. Much. Love.

Foreword

As you open this book, prepare to embark on a transformative adventure involving the most structured and insightful exploration of the Inner Critic I have encountered. The authors are not just scholars and practitioners with decades of professional experience bettering the lives of clients, they have also deeply lived the book's content.

This isn't a passive read; it's an immersive journey into the heart of self-awareness and compassion. Each chapter unfolds with powerful exercises designed to challenge and reshape the internal narratives that govern your emotions and actions. Imagine transforming that harsh inner voice, the one we all know too well, into a source of gentle encouragement that helps us attain the things we value most in life.

Shawn and Holly weave professional expertise and personal experiences into a rich tapestry, creating a resource dedicated to reader growth. Vulnerability about their own struggles with the Inner Critic injects authenticity and a sense of shared humanity into the process. This workbook is not just a guide—it is a loving hand that holds yours as you navigate the path to self-transformation together.

Through numerous, thoughtfully crafted exercises, you'll delve into the origins of your Inner Critic, understand its impact on your psyche and relationships, and develop strategies to manage its influence. You'll emerge equipped with skills to replace self-criticism with self-compassion, fostering emotional resilience and your capacity to vastly enrich your own life.

This interactive workbook is a treasure trove for anyone seeking significant, lasting personal growth. It's a proactive partner in the quest for self-improvement and engaging with its content promises a transformative experience—far exceeding the boundaries of traditional reading. Beyond simply offering tools, it provides wisdom for integrating them effectively into your life. The structured activities will spark potent and powerful self-reflection, paving the way for lasting positive change in how you view yourself and interact with the world.

Embark on this adventure with an open heart and a resolute mind, ready to rewrite your narrative within. The true power of this workbook comes from actively practicing its teachings.

The rich, engaging experience promises to lessen internal conflict, elevate self-esteem, and cultivate a life beyond criticism—guided by compassion and values.

This is more than a workbook, it's a wellspring of invaluable insights and practices with the potential to usher in a life brimming with joy and less burdened by suffering. As you turn each page, remember: the magic is in the practices that are waiting to be brought to life by you.

—Mavis Tsai, PhD
    Co-creator of Functional Analytic Psychotherapy; senior research scientist at the University of Washington; founder of Awareness, Courage & Love Global Project

Introduction

Sigh. It is difficult to live with a harsh, criticizing voice constantly sounding off in our minds! That voice picks at mistakes, compares us to others, and scolds us for doing the wrong thing—or not doing enough. It leaves us feeling that we are not *being* enough, that we will never be enough. The voice questions our worth. It generates thoughts and stories in our own mind that show up as criticism at best and nastiness at worst. Since you are reading this page, you may be like us—struggling with a critical voice, with all its thoughts and stories.

For this workbook, we are naming the voice that hurts us our *Inner Critic*. When, where, and how does this voice show up? It is powerful, and so often—too often—we do not even know where it comes from. It interferes with how we walk through the world. It keeps us stuck and robs us of our sense of value. It causes suffering in ways that interfere with our ability to engage in deep, meaningful relationships.

This voice and its stories have likely been with you for a long time. They may have served you once, but not anymore. If they were helping, you probably wouldn't be reading this book, and we wouldn't have felt compelled to write it.

In this book, you'll learn where the Inner Critic comes from, how it shows up, and ways it interferes with meaning and connection in your life. You'll explore compassion toward your critical self, as you learn why compassion is its antidote and the way to make lasting peace with your Inner Critic. By the end of this book, you'll understand how self-compassion works and why it works—and be able to incorporate self-compassion into your daily life.

Many wonderful authors and teachers on self-compassion, self-forgiveness, and self-love have written books. This is because there is no magic pill to take, or simple recipe to apply, that offers a one-and-done cure. Learning self-compassion is a process. Applying it, patiently and consistently, is a *practice*. You need to work at it. This is why we created this journey through an experiential workbook for you.

As you engage the practice of bringing compassion to your critic, your heart can open. You will learn how to care for yourself in big ways and small ways. Also, you'll begin extending the same kindness to yourself that you offer other people. Then you can discover deeper relationships with yourself and the people in your life. So, in this workbook, you will practice, practice, practice self-compassion—and then you will practice some more.

One of the reasons this book came to be is personal: we, the authors, let our Inner Critics run our lives for a very long time. Through our own personal and professional work, we have cultivated and applied skills and tools that help us through our pain and suffering. We now want to help reduce your suffering and we feel confident that when you can act on these tools and apply them to your life, as we and our clients have, you will indeed suffer less and gain hope that you can act on and apply to your life.

Professionally, as clinicians, we have amassed a lot of data that shows the effectiveness of the practices in this workbook. The therapeutic interventions we apply in our work with clients are also incorporated into this interactive journey. All in all, our work to extend the kindness to ourselves that nourishes self-worth, reduces shame, enhances connection in relationships— and quiets our Inner Critic—is now offered for you to do too.

Who Is This Workbook For?

This workbook is for anyone who wants to make significant and lasting changes to how they look at themselves, how they treat themselves, and how they are *willing* to treat themselves. It offers you a different way of looking at your life: moving from how you *have* been treating yourself to how you *could* be treating yourself—with self-compassion and a sense of agency as you seek the life you wish to live. It's not the limited life that the critic, and its fears, insists is all you're capable of creating.

You, like too many of us, may have trauma histories, difficult family dynamics, or past hurts that have fueled your critic's voice and contributed to how you see yourself. While painful, those experiences don't have to keep you from taking steps toward creating another way. We created this workbook to let you know that you are not alone in facing these kinds of painful histories.

What Does This Book Offer?

This book offers skills that will help you work through fear to discover a new way to live— coming from compassion and connection—that moves toward meaning and purpose. The tools are derived from acceptance and commitment therapy (ACT), functional analytic psychotherapy (FAP), compassion-focused therapy (CFT), and other therapies backed by science.

We'll explore the origins and functions of the Inner Critic in chapters 1, 2, and 3. Why is it there? What is it trying to help you do? How can you learn to work with it, rather than be ruled by it? From there, in chapter 4, we introduce self-compassion and offer ways you can use it to begin quieting that harsh inner voice. The remainder of the book shows you how to combine self-compassion with mindful awareness to transform your relationship with the Inner Critic. Chapter 5 introduces you to a tool for compassionate self-observation. Chapter 6 helps you learn to identify what you truly value—not what your critic tells you is important. Chapters 7 and 8 guide you through how to act according to your values, self-compassionately, in moments when things get tough.

You'll also develop techniques to keep the Inner Critic quiet and peaceful when it tends to get loudest. Through this journey, you will begin by finding out how this Inner Critic came to take up so much room in your life and then, in later chapters, you will tenderly, lovingly invite it to step aside. Ultimately, you will learn how to say *shhh*—with kindness—to the voice that has been hurting you for so long. As you will discover, it wants to help, but doesn't.

We suggest that you spend time each day reading and doing the exercises. Your life is busy and this is work. But this is important work. It is effort applied to quieting the demon we call the Inner Critic, so you can navigate your days armed with the kindness and self-compassion that ultimately leads to a richer, less sufferable, more joyful life.

Personally, we have made this work into a ritual. You can too. Consider fitting it in before your day starts, or perhaps at the end of your day if that's a better time. Whatever you decide, see if you can spend at least fifteen minutes doing an exercise or reading a chapter. Who knows, you may feel compelled to do more! Additional worksheets, tools, and audio recordings of guided meditations are available online at http://www.newharbinger.com/54292. Whatever time is spent, remember the promise is in the practice, and there is practice in the pages of this book.

Our Invitation to You

If you want to reduce the suffering that comes with the harsh Inner Critic, we extend an invitation. We invite you to meet yourself where you are and guide yourself to where you want to be, with compassion. Because truly, what is the alternative? The alternative is more of the same—more self-criticism, more limits, more emotional suffering. You have picked up this workbook because more of the same is no longer working.

We believe that YOU are worth the work. Specifically, working through the exercises will help you:

- give yourself a break by understanding that you are not at fault

- reduce the suffering that results from shame, anxiety, or depression

- foster a sense of worthiness, belonging, lovability, and connection

- identify whether an inner voice is helpful or hurtful

- connect, or reconnect, with what really matters to you and what brings purpose into your life

- cultivate the ability to choose to respond rather than react

- commit to active practice so you can expand your skills and flourish

- improve the quality of your relationships

- increase your ability to act with meaning and purpose

This book organizes strategies developed from the evidence-based work of leading self-compassion experts. We have adapted these ideas to create a practical and concise way of building skills into a mindful self-compassion practice. Using this framework has helped many of our clients and loved ones quiet their Inner Critic by giving them ways to cultivate compassion. We, ourselves, have used this framework with each other. Our promise to you, dear reader, is that these stories, examples, and exercises—the very ones that helped us, our loved ones, and our clients—will help you too.

With that, let's get started!

CHAPTER 1

We're Built to Be Hard on Ourselves

I talk too much. I'm so annoying.

I can't believe I just said that. They must think I'm such an idiot!

My teeth aren't straight—I'm so ugly.

Why can't I be normal and be more relaxed, so I know what to say?

F'ing loser. That's what I am.

I'm just hopeless.

Oh my god! Shut it! Stop being a crybaby and get over yourself!

If they really knew me…

I deserved it.

Sound familiar? That voice inside your head is giving you the play-by-play of all the things you do wrong, pointing out what you never do right and never will do right, shouting that you are not good enough, attractive enough, lovable enough. That voice tells you that you will never *be* enough. Your mind may not stop there. Perhaps it goes on to pummel you for being so hard on yourself: *Why am I doing this to myself? What is wrong with me?*

This happens to us too. What is that voice? Why is it so loud? Why can't we just stop talking to ourselves that way, especially when it feels so painful and destructive?

In this chapter, you'll learn what the Inner Critic is, and where it comes from. You'll identify when and how that voice shows up and explore why you think it's your fault, why you are unkind to yourself, and why you have such a hard time "getting past it."

It is not your fault that you think and feel this way. You actually ended up here honorably, because so many things contributed to the development of your Inner Critic. Maybe that sounds like rough news or offers relief. There are ways you can make peace with this Inner Critic and use its voice to fuel self-compassion and confidence. The first step to getting there is identifying how your critical inner voice shows up and where it comes from.

What Is the Inner Critic?

You have many chatty parts of your mind that produce thousands of thoughts each day. The Inner Critic is one voice among them. It serves up all sorts of negative thoughts, comparisons, judgments, insults, and stories about yourself—including your intentions, thoughts, actions, personal characteristics, and your worthiness as a lovable and capable human being. You might even mistake this voice as being one and the same as "me."

In general, when any of us is hit with a stream of thoughts like these and become aware of them, we criticize ourselves. While some types of self-critical behaviors lead to useful ends, this workbook focuses on the kind of self-criticism that is unproductive, is used in a sharp and hurtful way, and leads us away from living meaningful and satisfying lives.

Here are some more perspectives on what the self-critical voice is. Self-criticism is:

- "…the tendency to engage in negative self-evaluation that results in feelings of worthlessness, failure, and guilt when expectations are not met" (Naragon-Gainey and Watson 2012).

- harsh and punitive self-judgment and self-scrutiny (Shahar et al. 2011).

- "…constant and harsh self-scrutiny, overly critical evaluations of [our] own behavior, and negative reactions to perceived failures in terms of active self-bashing (Löw, Schauenburg, and Dinger 2020).

These are just some definitions of self-critical behavior. One common theme among them is that they all skew toward the negative. Consider how these definitions fit your experience.

Which definition sounds like a description of you? Had you known that self-criticism was a thing? If so, describe your experience of trying to work with it.

_____

_____

_____

Identify Your Self-Critical Behavior

Grasping a definition of self-critical behavior is easy; spotting it in real time is trickier. After all, the voice of your Inner Critic is so constant, habitual, and *familiar*, it can be difficult to discern it from other, more mundane thoughts. It might even be a dominant mode of thinking about yourself.

We often don't even know we are doing it! Until we feel the sting. This is what makes the Inner Critic so problematic. The painful feelings it brings up and our responses to them are *automatic*. We feel the hurt the Inner Critic generates and immediately act on it. Rather than letting those feelings drive our behavior without any awareness, we can begin to recognize this voice. With awareness of where and when self-critical behavior happens, we can instead *notice* and *label* how we are feeling—before we act.

The following exercise will help you increase your awareness of feelings. Negative ones typically indicate that the Inner Critic is present, so we'll focus on those. This exercise will also help you begin attending to the feelings and thoughts that arise in the present moment, and the ways these feelings and thoughts spur you to behave. The present moment is the only time when true change can happen. Spend some time with this exercise, as we'll build upon it throughout the workbook.

Exercise: Exploring Negative Emotions

Working through the exercises in this book, you may find that things get stirred up a bit—even a lot. This is to be expected. In this first exercise, we ask that you stretch further than your comfort zone, as much as you are able, while you begin to identify feelings.

Here is a list of fifty common negative emotions. There are plenty more than we listed, as we never seem to run out. Feel free to add your own. Circle the emotions you experience regularly in your day-to-day life.

Alarm	Insecurity	Self-consciousness
Anger	Isolation	Self-doubt
Anxiety	Jealousy	Self-loathing
Contempt	Loneliness	Shame
Dejection	Nauseated	Shock
Depression	Nervous	Sorrow
Disappointment	Numb	Stress
Disgust	Overwhelm	Stuckness
Dread	Panic	Tension
Embarrassment	Powerlessness	Uncertainty
Failure	Regret	Unease
Fatigue	Rejection	Vulnerability
Fear	Remorse	Worry
Frustration	Resentment	Worthlessness
Grief	Resignation	_____
Guilt	Restlessness	_____
Helplessness	Revulsion	_____
Humiliation	Sadness	_____

The circled emotions I most commonly experience include:

_____   _____   _____   _____

Next, choose one of the words you circled. In the space provided, list how it interferes with your life in the following ways. Here are examples of how Holly described the emotion "insecurity." She wrote:

Insecurity affects how I...

feel about myself: **It makes me feel not good enough and invisible.**

move through my life: **It makes me question everything I do, so I can't have any sense of ease or flow when completing tasks.**

interact with others: **Because it constantly tells me that I'm not good enough, insecurity stops me from engaging much with people, even though I deeply care about them.**

It's your turn. Choose one of the emotions you circled and ask yourself how that emotion makes you feel.

_____ affects how I...

feel about myself: _____

_____

_____

move through my life: _____

_____

_____

interact with others: _____

_____

_____

Now call to mind your earliest memory of this emotion. Where were you? What were you doing? Describe the experience.

_____

_____

_____

_____

Repeat this exercise for each of the emotions you circled in the list. You can download the Exploring Negative Emotions worksheet at http://www.newharbinger.com/54292 to print as many copies as you need.

Chances are, a lot of emotions came up for you in the last exercise that were painful. It's rough to be driven by your Inner Critic's voice. Whether you feel the need to escape it or obey it, the experience is negative.

Things that really matter to you probably came up too. For instance, maybe you feel "stuckness" at work, which reveals that your career and sense of pride in your work are things that matter to you. Or maybe "anxiety" and "stress" come up for you as a parent. This reveals how deeply you take the responsibility of parenting.

Pain is part of the price of admission for being a human being. As excruciating as feelings like insecurity, shame, self-loathing, and more, can seem, it's inevitable that they will arise in the course of caring for yourself and caring for others. Pain is as inevitable as the positive experiences of loving, dreaming, and living a life of meaning. But none of us need the self-punishment and shame of the Inner Critic. Instead, you can identify and change that harsh voice to find some self-kindness along the way.

Parts of You Targeted by the Inner Critic

The Inner Critic tends to focus its attention on where we are most vulnerable. It zeroes in on, and attacks, the parts of ourselves that are easily wounded, which we call *targets*. Paul Gilbert, the founder of compassion-focused therapy (CFT), identifies several key aspects of ourselves that the Inner Critic targets (Gilbert and Miles 2000). Among them are *physical appearance, emotions, personality,* and *intellectual characteristics.* These are not the only targets that your Inner Critic may be attacking. Let's take a look at what your own targets are.

Exercise: Identifying Your Targets

The following categories will help you identify what your Inner Critic targets. Consider each of these aspects of yourself and write down three specific examples of ways your Inner Critic attacks it.

My Physical Appearance

Example: **If I could just lose these last ten pounds, then I wouldn't be such a loser.**

1. _____
2. _____
3. _____

My Behaviors

Example: **I'm not doing enough; I should be doing more.**

1. _____
2. _____
3. _____

My Inner Thoughts

Example: **When I think that way about myself, it just proves that I'm a wreck.**

1. _____
2. _____
3. _____

My Emotions

Example: I'm too sensitive. Everyone else can handle things just fine.

1. _____
2. _____
3. _____

My Personality

Example: If I could just be different, like everyone else, people would like me.

1. _____
2. _____
3. _____

My Intellectual Characteristics

Example: If people really knew me, they'd know I'm not so smart after all.

1. _____
2. _____
3. _____

My _____

1. _____
2. _____
3. _____

My _____

1. _____

2. _____

3. _____

Look over your lists. Do you notice any common themes? Does your Inner Critic pick at everything? Does it target specific aspects of yourself that are particularly tender? Write your observations down.

_____

_____

_____

_____

_____

_____

_____

How are you doing as you read and do the exercises? Check in with yourself often throughout this process so you can reach that deep place inside of you where the Inner Critic lives. Here's a brief exercise that's helpful to practice any time you need to slow down, sit with strong feelings, or think through any of the material throughout this book. For now, simply bring curiosity and openness as you give it a try. This exercise will repeat throughout this workbook as a reminder that it can be practiced as often as needed—even several times a day.

Exercise: Listening to Your Self-Compassionate Voice

We invite you to put a hand on your heart, breathe in, and ask yourself: *How am I in this moment?* Then listen. What is your intuitive voice saying? Whatever it says, whatever comes up for you matters. Write down what came up for you during this check in.

_____

_____

_____

_____

_____

_____

Through this exercise, we applaud your willingness to embrace vulnerability. You may notice some unpleasant, or even painful, feelings right now. Make room for those feelings—they are telling you something. Maybe something important. Listening to how you feel and accepting how you feel is the beginning of a self-compassion practice. It is the most effective way to cope with the Inner Critic. In chapters 4 and 5, you'll learn a lot more about self-compassion.

Where Does Your Inner Critic Come From?

How did this critical inner voice even come to be? It's a harsh and unwanted voice that leaves us feeling hurt, stuck, and unhappy with ourselves. So why do we allow it to guide us through life?

As humans, from the start, we are destined to develop a self-critical voice. Period. There. We said it. It's part of how we're built. The structures in our brains respond to certain types of information, which influences how we respond to various situations. The Inner Critic's voice comes from one of those responses.

Your early relationship with your family, as well as with your teachers, peers, social networks, and environment all influence how you learn to talk to yourself. Humans learn through observation and imitation, behaviors that are reinforced or punished, and language. You are influenced by words themselves, how you use them, and the stories and rules you were taught.

There are multiple ways this voice came to have meaning and become so powerful in your life. What's most important to know is that your Inner Critic is a part of you. It did not come out of nowhere; you didn't invent it nor are you imagining it. It is also not unique to you; it is not something that you experience because you are weak in ways other people are not. You aren't doing anything wrong, and you are not broken because you experience it.

You may have wondered at times why your Inner Critic seems so much louder than everyone else's, why others seem to move through their lives with much more ease than you. If this is your experience, you are not alone! Each person has a unique combination of factors that contribute to what their own critic sounds like. And we all have learned to interact with it in different ways. Let's look at the following prevalent factors fueling our Inner Critic. We'll spend the rest of this chapter discussing and exploring:

- your threat-detection system

- how you bonded with early caregivers

- what you learned through consequences

- the ways observation and imitation affect you

- how you use language

- the rules and behavioral expectations you grew up with

- the stories you tell yourself

Your Threat-Detection System

Your brain includes structures that automatically respond to physical danger by activating processes designed to keep you safe. You may have heard this threat-defense system called the *fight-or-flight response* (Cannon 1915) and you likely have experienced it. Here's an example of what it is designed to do. Say you're driving and an animal suddenly darts in front of your car. Your arm muscles tense and automatically swerve the steering wheel in the direction opposite the animal; you experience warmth and butterflies in your belly; your armpits get sweaty and your heart begins to pound. Emotionally, you feel anger and fear, disgust, or a state of disbelief. This all occurs instantly and without conscious choice.

Your threat-defense system is one of the oldest functions of your brain and is always on the lookout for danger. When it senses danger, it instantly prepares your body to do what it needs in order to put up a defense as quickly as possible. Time is of the essence, and this system bypasses time-consuming conscious thought to instantly prepare you to be strong and fast. It does this by sending out chemical messengers directly to the necessary body parts. Your experience of this process can include an unpleasant physical and emotional tension—the need to *do* something. Part of this "wiring" is the urge to reduce or eliminate that unpleasant tension. By so doing, you avoid or evade a threat.

The emotions you experience at the time likely correspond to what your body is doing. *Fight* responses are confrontational and may be experienced as anger. *Flee* responses involve getting away from danger and correspond with fear or disgust. *Freeze* responses correspond with a paralysis or numbing of emotions as a means to "become invisible" to the danger. *Fawn* responses are behaviors that we engage in to minimize threat by pleasing and appeasing (Walker 2013). Your threat-defense system will read the situation and respond in whatever way seems best to keep you safe.

This is a very helpful process to have within—it can be lifesaving, at times! Unfortunately, for many of us, it develops into an unhelpful *pattern of behavior*. Because the threat-defense system is constantly scanning your environment for threats, it notices anything that could possibly be threatening. But sometimes these threats aren't *actual* threats—they're *perceived* ones. Unlike other animals, humans can feel threatened not only by dangers in our external world but by perceived threats inside ourselves, as well. Distressing thoughts, disturbing memories and images, and painful emotions all have the potential to activate the threat-defense system because they make you feel uncomfortable. This discomfort might be read as a threat to your well-being and can trigger attempts to neutralize or eliminate those threats via fight, flight, freeze, or fawn responses.

Throughout the course of our lives, we may have those internal experiences for all sorts of reasons other than actual physical threats. Once the threat-defense system associates those things with danger, it becomes more and more likely we'll respond to them *as if they are* danger. We may try to neutralize or eliminate them whenever they arise. This may result in even *more* painful or distressing thoughts, feelings, images, or memories, which requires more defense behaviors. And so on. Over time, a sustained pattern develops: we always respond to uncomfortable internal experiences in threat mode.

When you have thoughts, emotions, and memories that feel threatening or distressing, you may fight them, evade them, become paralyzed, attempt to appease them, or try to avoid situations that trigger those experiences. All this, in service of avoiding "danger." You are, in essence, struggling and defending against yourself.

You certainly want your threat-response system to react to real physical danger. Unfortunately, it often responds to situations that are not physically threatening. This exercise invites you to explore your own threat system and how it might be activating your Inner Critic.

Exercise: Your Threat System and Your Body

Take a moment to read through the following instructions and then close your eyes and try to fully imagine the experience before writing your responses. Think back to a time when you were in some sort of danger or at immediate risk of being injured. Crashing on your bicycle. Being startled by a bear on a camping trip. Finding yourself alone at night in an unfamiliar place. Briefly describe what was going on.

_____

_____

_____

_____

_____

_____

_____

_____

_____

Now recall the physical experience you had. Really breathe into the memory, take some time, and notice how the experience affected your body. Consider the following list and check all the experiences that apply, adding more of your own at the end of the exercise.

When this happened, my body responded with:

☐ tense muscles

☐ rapid or shallow breathing

☐ holding breath

☐ rapid heart rate

☐ feeling "butterflies" or "a pit" in the stomach

☐ sweating

☐ suddenly feeling very hot or cold

☐ clammy hands

☐ raised blood pressure

☐ throbbing temples or headache

☐ tunnel vision or foggy vision

☐ stomach pains

☐ nausea

☐ urge to go to the bathroom

☐ urge to leave where you are

☐ tearfulness or crying

☐ irritability or anger

☐ emotional numbness

☐ poor concentration

☐ hypervigilance

☐ difficulty finding words

☐ difficulty remembering things about this situation

☐ _____

☐ _____

☐ _____

Notice how you are feeling. Are you experiencing any of those sensations now? Are you also able to notice that you are *remembering* something that happened? The situation that happened *then* is not happening *now*. It isn't really here and you aren't in it. Yet your body is responding as if the bear is in the room with you right now!

As we shared, when you are actually safe but experiencing distressing emotions, your threat-detection system can kick in as if there is physical danger. Here's an exercise that will help you explore how this works.

Exercise: Your Threat System and Your Emotions

Think over the last couple of weeks and recall a time when you experienced a really distressing or painful emotion. Not a dangerous situation, like you did in the previous exercise. This is an experience that caused you to feel upset—perhaps a painful social situation or something harsh your Inner Critic said to you.

Briefly describe what was going on.

_____

_____

_____

_____

Now, again, take some time to notice what your body was doing. Refer to the checklist for the previous exercise, then circle any sensations that you experienced when recalling this emotional reaction.

Afterward, notice how you are feeling. Are you experiencing any of those sensations right now? Once again, you are *remembering* something that happened. That situation occurred *then* and it is not happening *now*. It isn't really here with you in the room. Yet your body may still be responding, even now, to this memory of discomfort, as if that doggone bear is in the room with you right now!

In the moment, you may not be fully aware that this kind of a response is happening or why. This is the reason why one of the first steps of changing your relationship to the Inner Critic is increasing awareness. While you may be hardwired for your threat system and self-critic to react, when you can anticipate how your Inner Critic shows up, you'll begin to predict it. That's when you'll have options for how to respond in more helpful, kind ways.

Soon we'll look at other ways we ended up where we are. But first, it's a good time to pause and practice listening to your self-compassionate voice.

Exercise: Listening to Your Self-Compassionate Voice

Put your hand on your heart, breathe in, and ask yourself, *How am I in this moment?* Now listen. What is your intuitive self saying? Whatever comes up for you matters. Write down what you hear.

_____

_____

_____

_____

_____

Your Bonds with Early Caregivers

How we do or don't bond with our caregivers is called *attachment style*. Attachment Theory, developed by psychologist John Bowlby, emphasizes how the quality of our early relationships influences our behaviors throughout the course of our lives. Bowlby defined *attachment* as a "lasting psychological connectedness between human beings" (Bowlby 1969). By considering the quality of your individual attachments to caregivers, you'll gain insight into how your ability to connect with other people influences how you relate to yourself.

All children are born with a need to bond with their caregivers. How caregivers respond during the formation of those bonds can determine how children learn to interact with others and themselves. For example, an absent or neglectful caregiver who doesn't express love and affection toward their child may leave the child wondering what is wrong with them. Often, children assume the blame, believing they are unlovable as a result of something they did wrong. They can even think a caregiver's neglect reflects some inherent flaw or fault in them. Let's look at an example of this.

When Jennifer completed the exercise Exploring Negative Emotions, she identified that she experiences *self-doubt* and *overwhelming uncertainty* a lot. "I never feel good enough," Jennifer wrote. "I'm not ever sure if what I'm doing is okay or right. I always feel like I'm in trouble. It makes me wonder how I even matter to other people, so I wind up isolating myself from everyone—which makes me feel worse." Read the following story and see if you can identify the role Jennifer's attachment style, forged in childhood, played in her life as she grew up and how it continues to play out now.

Jennifer's parents divorced when she was twelve and her sister was ten years old. Before the divorce, their household was chaotic, with loud arguments that would sometimes turn volatile. Jennifer and her sister turned to friends and their families for emotional safety. When her parents divorced, her mother moved with her daughters to another state, which meant a new school, new people, and no feeling of emotional safety. Jennifer and her sister only had each other.

In their household, there was never physical abuse, and they were both provided for monetarily, so the message was, "Not only are you fine, but you're lucky." Yet, what was confusing was that they did not feel fine or lucky. Their mother's mood and behavior could change on a dime. In fact, they never quite knew who they would get when they walked into the house. Would Mom be the loving parent who wanted to be friends? Would she be the emotionally dysregulated Mom who screamed and blamed the girls for how her life had turned out? Would she be the emotionally inconsolable Mom they rallied around and took care of?

While her sister learned to disappear, literally leaving the house to travel with her soccer team, Jennifer learned that her value was based on how much she could help and soothe her mom. Because things were never soothed and fixed for very long, the narrative "I am not enough" became the driving voice in her head. Flying under the radar became a very useful way to escape Mom's moods. But Jennifer's own emotions were invalidated and dismissed. As a result, there was a lot of loneliness and emptiness in their household, and no feeling of belonging anywhere.

Given this history, it makes sense that Jennifer's Inner Critic shows up in ways that make her doubt herself and question how and where she fits in. Feeling uncertain, being full of self-doubt, and flying under the radar were behaviors that kept Jennifer *safe* at one time. But that was then. Now, this way of moving through the world interferes with how she *wants* to see herself. She longs for a sense of self-worth and belonging. However, the Inner Critic tells her she has to be better. It constantly reminds Jennifer that she is not good enough and doesn't really matter. Let's explore your own experience of how early bonds with caregivers influenced your attachment.

Exercise: Attachment

What kind of early bonds did you have? Based upon what you remember your experience was like most of the time as a child, answer the following questions about your relationships with caregivers.

Who were the people in your immediate family when you were a child? Who lived in the home with you?

_____

_____

_____

For each of the following pairs of words, circle the word that best describes how you felt most of the time.

safe / unsafe

loved / rejected

secure / uncertain

connected / alone

heard / ignored

trusted / doubted

validated / judged

When you were hurt, scared, or upset, did you go to anyone for comfort? If so, describe how they helped. If not, what did you do for comfort?

_____

_____

_____

_____

Write about how your caregivers responded when you...

made a mistake. _____

_____

expressed strong emotions. _____

_____

expressed a need. _____

_____

There are usually deep connections between your childhood attachments and how your self-critic talks to you now. What connections or patterns do you see?

_____

_____

_____

_____

_____

There are a number of ways to look at how the Inner Critic comes to be and why it says the things it typically says. In addition to your attachments with caregivers, you also learned to respond to your world in other ways. Let's look at some of them now.

Learning Through Consequences and Imitation

Two common ways we learn to respond to the world are through the *consequences* of our behaviors, which often go on to shape how we behave in the future, and through *imitation* or *social learning*, where we pick up behaviors by observing what's been modeled for us. We'll explore them both in turn.

CONSEQUENCES

Our actions are based on previous behaviors, which behavioral psychologist B. F. Skinner called *operant conditioning* (Skinner 1938). This type of learning occurs when a behavior is influenced by conditions that follow it, so when a behavior is followed by favorable consequences or reinforcement, the behavior increases. When a behavior is followed by negative consequences or punishment, the behavior decreases. Consider Claire's experience.

Claire is a middle-aged woman feeling extremely depressed and anxious, and also very bad about herself. In childhood, whenever she had a need and tried to express it, like feeling hungry and needing either dinner or a snack, she was often reprimanded. The response was similar when she expressed feelings—especially negative ones like frustration, impatience, sadness, or fear—as she was verbally, physically, and emotionally punished by her parents. They called her names and criticized her. The only times she ever received praise from them was when she did well in school. Claire learned that having and expressing needs and feelings were dangerous and unacceptable behaviors. She also learned that when she stayed out of sight, "under the radar," and demonstrated that she had no needs—like not reminding her mother about dinner when it was forgotten —she learned she could be "safe." Growing up, this was acceptable and desirable behavior. She also learned that excelling in her studies earned her attention and praise, which led her to overwork as an adult. But Claire *did have needs and feelings* and learned to believe that she was therefore never "doing things right" or "good enough" to earn her parents' love.

OBSERVATION AND IMITATION

Another way learning shaped your self-critical voice is via the behaviors you learned through observation and imitation. Albert Bandura, another research psychologist interested in how we learn, developed Social Learning Theory, which focuses on how we learn by observing and imitating others. Bandura's research emphasizes that *self-efficacy*—our ability to perform tasks with skill and confidence—is shaped by positive reinforcement from others and leads to more intrinsic feelings of skill and mastery (Bandura and Walters 1977).

While there is a lack of consensus about exactly how learning happens in this context, it is clear that observation and imitation have powerful effects on our lives. Especially in formative years, watching how others manage their needs, handle their feelings, and treat themselves and others teaches us how to manage our own needs and feelings.

Starting at an early age, children are highly tuned-in to others' behaviors, whether observed directly, described, or viewed through media such as television, books, or online platforms. Children are especially curious about the behaviors of people like themselves, or people they perceive to have high status, be holders of knowledge, or serve as nurturing figures. By observing how these "models" respond to the world, and how the world responds in kind, children learn vicariously what consequences their behaviors might elicit. Let's look at what Alex learned.

> Alex came to therapy because he struggled with addictive behaviors that interfered with his ability to have a long-term intimate relationship, be sober and alert at work, and think of his future beyond the latest obsession or fix. As a young child, his parents argued constantly about his father's extended absences. While his mother eventually moved herself, Alex, and his brother out of the house, the kids were still required to see their father weekly. During these visits, their father mostly ignored Alex and his brother and left them alone in front of the TV. There was rarely any food available until he returned, which was sometimes well after midnight. On the rare occasions he stayed home, the boys witnessed their father drinking excessively and watching pornography. When they did talk, their father mostly blamed their mother for the divorce and his miserable lot in life.
>
> Through therapy, Alex saw that he had learned to avoid difficult feelings and emotions through sexually addictive behaviors, lack of personal responsibility, blaming others, and also neglecting the people in his life. He had adopted the very same ineffective behaviors he had observed his father using to manage his own suffering.

Now it's your turn to consider how you learned to manage your own needs and emotions by watching other people's behavior.

Exercise: What You Observed and Imitated

Identify the key people you spent time with as an elementary-school-aged child:

parents and caregivers _____

_____

older siblings _____

_____

school and play peer group _____

_____

school and play peer group's caregivers and families _____

_____

others _____

_____

Next, given what you learned from consequences and imitation, when you think about how your Inner Critic talks to you now, where else have you heard that voice and its harsh messages? Who used that tone of voice, said those hurtful things...to you? To themselves? To others?

_____

_____

_____

_____

_____

_____

Observation and imitation are yet two more examples of how we, as humans, are bound to develop self-critical behaviors. Next, we'll explore another behavior—our use of language—that also has a significant role in the development of the critical voice.

How You Use Language

Would it surprise you to learn that words do, in fact, matter? You have learned that your mind is always on the lookout for threats. To do that, it is ever-busy relating events, people, and actions around you to categories of good or bad, safe or dangerous. The Inner Critic itself arises from how that part of your mind uses language, through a process of deriving meaning from all that it encounters. In this way, it can give you basic rules for living that will keep you safe. Or that's the idea anyway.

What this boils down to is that the words we use have impacts well beyond sharing information with others; they also have huge implications for how we relate to ourselves. One theory of language, known as relational frame theory (RFT), suggests that how we learn and use language has a role in the development of unhelpful behaviors (Hayes, Barnes-Holmes, and Roche 2001), including self-criticism. Let us explain.

Early in human development, we learn to use language to describe and make sense of the world. Words are symbols for objects and people not present, such as dog, mother, ball. Often, infants are taught language directly by caregivers. Imagine a parent pointing to a furry animal with whiskers and a long tail and saying the word "cat." Their child, Lucia, learns that the word cat *means, is the same as*, that animal. What's extraordinary about human language learning is that we don't always have to be directly taught. We have the capacity to derive, or make connections, to figure something out.

Consider this example: Lucia's grandmother speaks Spanish, and when she points to the cat, she says the word "gato." Lucia has been directly taught that *gato* means, *is the same as*, that animal. What Lucia is not directly taught, but is able to *derive*, is that "cat" is the same as "gato." She is able to fill in the blanks, so to speak. Sometimes, however, deriving isn't helpful. Let's say that Lucia meets the neighbor's cat and that cat scratches her. It hurts! As her parent dries Lucia's tears and bandages her arm, she says "Ouch!" After that, Lucia is cautious around all cats—both the neighbor's cat and her grandmother's cat. She has derived this experience that all cats can "ouch" and should therefore be avoided. This response is probably helpful sometimes, but other times, it takes away Lucia's opportunity to learn that some cats are nice and cuddly. The reason for this is that your protective languaging mind works fast, judges things as more threatening than they probably are, and alerts you to those potential risks harshly.

Where does the Inner Critic fit in? Let's look at what happens when you apply this same process of deriving to abstract concepts such as personal qualities. Your Inner Critic uses it against you.

A helpful way to see how this works is to consider how this principle operates with common experiences you may have had in your life. Here are five situations that demonstrate how we use language that can lead to self-criticism. Fill in the blank with what your mind comes up with.

Situation 1

Dad said lazy people are bad.

My teacher told me I was lazy.

I am _____.

Situation 2

Successful people always do their best.

I didn't do my best.

I am _____.

Situation 3

Strong people don't cry.

I cried.

I am _____.

Situation 4

Mistakes mean failure.

I made a mistake.

I am _____.

Situation 5

My anxiety in social situations is very uncomfortable.

Feeling uncomfortable is bad and needs to be fixed.

My anxiety is _____.

Do you recognize in these examples how your Inner Critic "fills in the blanks"? What are other situations in which your Inner Critic fills in the blanks?

_____

_____

_____

_____

_____

_____

Another feature of how humans use language to "fill in the blanks" is the ability to relate one thing to another. We can see how Lucia *relates* the words "cat" and "gato" with each other and the furry animal. That relation is "sameness." We can also learn other ways to relate, such as difference ("cat" does not mean "dog"), or comparison (dogs are bigger than cats). Humans are very good at learning to make associations in this way. As we expand and increase our interactions with the world, we infer, or "fill in the blanks," to create relations among many increasingly complex objects and abstract concepts. By adulthood, humans can, and do, relate anything to anything. Even when it doesn't make sense. We are masters at bending language to create a relation plausible enough that we believe it as if it were true. And we become so good at it that it becomes second nature. We do it on autopilot, outside of intentional awareness.

First, try your hand at "relating," and then we'll explain how this preferred language of the Inner Critic becomes so destructive.

Exercise: Exploring the Effects of Language

Let's play a word game. Write down your responses to the following question.

How is a floor lamp the grandfather of a cell phone?

_____

_____

What did you come up with? Did your clever mind offer ways in which it could seem possible that an inanimate object could be a "grandfather" to another inanimate object? Some people say something like, "A floor lamp uses an older technology that was a predecessor to the technology used for a cellphone. It's *as if* it is a grandfather." See how your mind made that story up? Created a made-up relationship that *seems* real? Lamps aren't grandfathers, yet we can talk about them *as if* they are. But it isn't really happening. *As if it is,* isn't the same thing as *it is*.

Here's another example: Write down your response to the following question.

Which color is better, green or orange?

_____

_____

We can create a relation, in this case a comparison, between two things because we can *verbally*. Just because we *can* do it, doesn't mean the words are "true." There is no "better" color in this example. Colors are not better or worse than another. They are just colors. And yet this verbal trick of putting them in an order of goodness leads us to believe, on automatic pilot, *as if* one color is better than another.

How often have you related your self-perception with what you have *derived* about yourself through language? When the message you hear is, "We are winners in this family and if you don't get those grades or get into this school, then you are not a winner." Our minds then tell us that, *If I am not a winner, I must be a loser.* You take that message to heart, *as if* it is true. We want to remind you that *as if* is not the same as *it is*. Remind yourself that the language of the Inner Critic is language that pits you against yourself. It doesn't have to be bought into and believed. Knowing this is another step toward quieting the voice of the Inner Critic.

Beginning to get the hang of it? Are you able to see how your mind automatically wants to create relationships where they don't exist? And then use that "truth" to punish you? Can you add a few more examples of how you do this?

_____

_____

_____

_____

RULES AND EXPECTATIONS YOU GREW UP WITH

You learned certain behaviors because you were taught rules about them. In fact, we are taught many rules passed down through families, communities, cultures, and society. Some rules aim to keep us physically safe while others might be intended to prevent us from feeling emotional distress. These latter rules are the ones your Inner Critic tends to uphold. Unlike learning to engage in behaviors more or less depending on what happens before and after we do them, we sometimes do or don't act simply depending on the rules we have learned about those behaviors. Most of us have never been attacked by a lion. We have been taught a rule, "Do not climb into the lion enclosure at the zoo or you may be mauled," and so we don't do it, despite never having experienced the negative consequence of being attacked by a lion. What about "Don't dart into the street without looking"?

Other examples of rule-governed behavior might be the thoughts "Always keep your feelings to yourself, otherwise you'll be seen as weak" and "It is unhealthy and abnormal to feel anxiety." What if…some of those rules that are passed down and taken for granted are actually not helpful? Novel concept!

Reflect on some rules that guide your thinking, feeling, and action. In this exercise, you'll ask: Are those rules limiting your life? Are they no longer serving the functions they once did? Are they not really workable long term? Let's dive in.

Exercise: Your Inner Critic's Rules and Expectations

Here are some common rules that your Inner Critic may be enforcing. Which of these rules were you taught to follow? Feel free to add more to the list.

You must be perfect.

Correct all mistakes.

Keep the peace at all costs.

Be nice.

Do your best; then do better.

If you don't have anything nice to say, don't say anything at all.

Failure is not an option.

You can do anything if you are dedicated enough.

There's always someone worse off than you, so count your blessings.

_____

_____

_____

Write about where you learned these rules. Who said these things to you? Are there any rules specific to your culture that have been emphasized in your family or community?

_____

_____

_____

_____

_____

_____

Now fill in the blanks with the rules that your Inner Critic most often, or most rigidly, insists you follow.

I should _____

I should _____

I should _____

I should not _____

I should not _____

I should not _____

You may be beginning to see how our use of language, and how we use it to make comparisons and construct rules, shape how our Inner Critic speaks to us.

The Stories You Tell Yourself

We are always creating narratives, or stories, in our own minds about events, situations, ourselves, and others. These stories form in childhood based on the factors you have learned about throughout this chapter: your overactive threat-detection system, learning how you impact the world and how the world shapes your behavior, observing other people, the way you learned to use language, and the rules and expectations you grew up with, among others. These stories are subjective interpretations, not necessarily objective facts. All the same, they can determine how you perceive and react to situations.

These harmful narratives came from outside of you. You have integrated them internally, until they became your own voice. Why? It didn't occur to your younger self that perhaps the people who were unintentionally helping you form these painful narratives…were wrong. It's not helpful to get stuck blaming or resenting them. Consider that they may have been trying to help you or were doing the best they knew how. Perhaps the painful messages resulted from the way they were raised or their own difficulty with negative and painful emotions. Maybe they thought this was the way to teach life lessons and help you develop a thick skin. You may never really know their reason.

What you do know is that their messages have resulted in the kind of hurt that becomes part of your own self-identification and can even hinder your development as a person. This deep wounding creates and compounds ongoing suffering. Rather than placing blame, knowing where your critical inner voices came from will help you transform them into a wiser, self-compassionate voice.

Your childhood stories can remain with you into adulthood, but they're tricky to rely on. For example, nine-year-old you may have adopted the narrative that if you were better looking, more people would like you. If at twenty-nine years old, you still believe this, you might be making some unhealthy decisions about your appearance in an effort to gain love. When your Inner Critic is involved, these stories can negatively affect the way you see yourself. That's why the adage "We are not our stories" resonates so widely. But our stories are important. They tell a tale about a specific time in our lives when hurt was happening.

Your stories give your suffering meaning. Your stories give your suffering context. Your stories *do* matter. *And* it's also true that what happened to you then is more than likely not happening now. Recognize that there are stories ingrained in the fabric of who you are. They remind you of the rules you were taught and were expected to follow; of the situations and relationships that reinforced the original, painful messages you were given about yourself. Let's look at the painful ones, so you are able to see how you can change your relationship to them. What would it be like if your stories didn't cause you to suffer the way you do?

We'll start by thinking of these stories as representing your *history* as an individual. That is, they're neither transcendent narratives that will always rule your life, nor relics of the past that you can simply shuck off if you choose to. By referring to your stories as your history, you can look back on painful times and the sense of yourself that arose from your pain to care for yourself. There are ways of recognizing these histories *and* opening up your heart that allow compassion to pour in. In this open space, you can behave how you want to behave. You can then begin to live the story you want.

For example, recall Jennifer's history of having to put her mother's needs before her own and keep her feelings to herself while she tended to her mother's emotions. As a grown woman, she still worries she will always get in trouble for whatever happens that causes someone else distress. Considering her own story, she identifies as someone who is overlooked and goes unnoticed, unless there is distress—then she is expected to tend to other people's emotions. She recognizes that while this was very much part of her experience as a child, it is not happening now—not in the same way. There may be times when she is in some way overlooked. But she knows that happens to everyone sometimes, and the reason it is particularly painful for her is because that is how she felt so much of the time growing up.

Now it's your turn to retell your story. Understanding and embracing your history will help you avoid identifying with it so closely that it becomes a trap. It'll help you use your history as a catalyst for self-compassion and prompt action that will help you be the person you want to be.

Exercise: Writing Your History

Go back in time to see how some of your life story has shaped your self-critical voice. In the space below or in a journal, we invite you to write your history. Include how it functioned then and how it's functioning now. What were the circumstances that got you here? Write as much, or as little, as you need to gain clarity.

How my history happened then: _____

_____

_____

_____

_____

_____

_____

_____

_____

_____

_____

_____

How this history is functioning in my life now: _____

_____

_____

_____

_____

_____

_____

_____

_____

_____

_____

_____

Now that you know where the Inner Critic came from, it is likely becoming clearer that having a harsh Inner Critic is *not your fault*. We all have an Inner Critic as part of our brains and learning history. Like you, many of us experience circumstances that shape and drive a critical inner voice. While sometimes this can help us ignore what's difficult in the short term, it leads us to suffer in the long term. Beginning to treat yourself with gentle understanding is the first step toward developing self-compassion.

We can't say it enough: You can quiet that critic. You can transform the inner voice you most often hear so it has a kind and compassionate tone. Let's check in with your compassionate voice.

Exercise: Listening to Your Self-Compassionate Voice

Put your hand on your heart, breathe in, and ask yourself, *How am I in this moment?* Now listen. What is your intuitive self saying? Write down what came up for you during this check in.

_____

_____

_____

_____

_____

_____

_____

_____

_____

_____

Having an inner voice that leaves you feeling bad about yourself and in emotional pain is an entirely common struggle. You have come to live with an Inner Critic for many reasons, including how you're built, how you learned to respond to your world, and how you use language. The more you learn about your Inner Critic and understand how it operates, the less you are at its mercy; the more you're able to make peace with it, the more inspired you'll be to create room for your feelings so they work better for you and hurt you less. In the next chapter, we'll explore how your Inner Critic tricks you with its promises to relieve your pain and we'll help you acknowledge its actual impact—causing you more pain. When you learn to clearly identify how your Inner Critic hurts you and holds you back, you'll gain more freedom to respond in ways that help you live with intention.

CHAPTER 2

So You Think That Critical Voice Is Helping You?

All of us have a critical inner voice. Listening to the Inner Critic and acting on messages that negatively target who we are leaves us feeling defeated by painful emotions. We are not even intentionally choosing it, so *why do we still listen to it?*

At some point, you learned to believe that all of the critical feedback helps you in some way. Maybe sometimes it even *is* helpful. In this chapter, we'll look at how the critic functions to determine if, and when, it actually is helpful—and when it is not.

Your Inner Critic's Function

Ultimately, our behaviors always make sense—in that they serve, or have served, some kind of function. Even behaviors we think of as "dysfunctional" can serve a function of some kind, when viewed in context. For example, lashing out angrily may be an understandable, if not entirely productive, response to a need that's gone unmet. Pulling an all-nighter can be an understandable way of driving yourself to complete something you feel obligated to do well. Staying quiet about your needs may be an understandable response in a situation where it doesn't feel safe to voice those needs. Thinking back on what you learned in chapter 1—about your threat detection system, your attachment with caregivers, and how rules, expectations, and language shaped the story you tell yourself—can you see how your behaviors make sense?

What functions have your behaviors served when you look at them in context? Reflect on this.

_____

_____

_____

_____

_____

The context of a situation helps us see the bigger picture of our behaviors. Let's do the same for your Inner Critic to see how helpful it actually is.

Exercise: When Does the Critic Show Up?

In chapter 1, you completed an exercise focusing on *how* the critic shows up for you. In this exercise, we are inviting you to take a look at *when* the critic shows up for you. In what situations; in what *context?*

Write about the situations in which you are most likely to hear from your inner critical voice. Include a life domain with each situation, choosing from the following options: parenting, self, social, tasks, work. Consider Shawn's examples.

Parenting: When my son does a dumb teenager thing, I think that I have failed as a parent.

Self: Making mistakes or failing at something means I am a failure.

Social: My Inner Critic shows up whenever I'm feeling ignored, minimized, dismissed, or rejected.

Tasks: My self-critic gets loud to keep me moving toward a goal like finishing a work project, running a race, and doing a hard workout.

Work: I'm critical when the stakes feel high and I'm doing something important, to me or to clients.

Now you give it a try. For each life domain, describe the circumstances when the Inner Critic speaks loudest.

Parenting: _____

_____

Self: _____

_____

Social: _____

_____

Tasks: _____

_____

Work: _____

_____

In what situations does your critic show up the most?

_____

_____

Consider any themes or patterns across life domains. What are they?

_____

_____

_____

_____

Ways You Expect the Critic to Help

As you were learning about life, you likely came to expect your self-critic to help you in a number of ways. You may expect it to keep you "safe" from emotional pain, to prevent mistakes, to toughen you up, to simplify decisions, to be included and ranked within a group, to compare yourself to others, and to motivate you to stay on task. Let's take a deeper look at some of these functions.

Keeping You Safe from Unwanted Emotions

Emotions are data. They provide information. They are not good or bad; they are a guide to how we can show up for ourselves and our experiences. The problem comes because the "bad" ones *feel* so "bad." They're often activated by environments in which you expected to be safe, like in your family home or with people you love. Because of that unmet expectation, you might define yourself as unlovable or unworthy or undeserving—or any of the "uns" you come up with.

Our shared culture furthers this dilemma and really solidifies it. We don't live in a culture that makes room for feeling bad. Instead, it promotes thinking "good" thoughts all the time and urges us to get rid of the hard, painful, yucky ones right away. Maybe you've heard things like "Stop that stinkin' thinkin'" or "Choose positive." The problem with that approach is yucky feelings don't go away for very long. They tend to come roaring back, typically more painful than before. When you are chronically cycling through painful feelings and your unsuccessful attempts to get rid of them, you may start thinking that you are the reason you feel this way. This plants the seed for your Inner Critic to barrage you with distracting critical judgments and stories about yourself. And you never get the information about situations, people, places, or your own needs that the painful feelings were signaling about in the first place.

In chapter 1, we shared how you are hardwired to avoid danger and how you learned rules that assume painful emotions are bad for you, maybe even dangerous, to encourage you to live in ways that avoid painful experiences. Imagine your Inner Critic commenting on a situation that is causing you emotional pain. Maybe it's the pain of guilt, failure, or disapproval and rejection. Your self-critical voice, wired from birth to save you from that pain, is going to try to rescue you. Not by whispering, *Hey, don't feel sad*—but by shouting, *Stop feeling sad and sorry for yourself! None of that! Nope, quit it right now!*

Write down three emotionally painful situations you find yourself in.

1. _____

2. _____

3. _____

In each of these situations, what does your Inner Critic shout at you?

1. _____

2. _____

3. _____

One reason you let the Inner Critic shout at you like this is because avoiding emotional pain seems helpful. Two things about that strategy don't work. First, the critic talks in ways that demean and demoralize you, causing far more devastating and enduring emotional pain than whatever is happening in the moment. Second, avoiding emotional pain isn't ultimately as helpful as it seems! A rich and vital life has pain in it. When you have zero tolerance for pain and turn your back on it, you are often turning your back on meaningful moments and turning away from a meaningful life.

While your Inner Critic is helping you stay "safe" by avoiding unwelcome negative emotions, those emotions are valid and natural and normal. They're just as valid and worthy of your attention as positive emotions.

Preventing You from Making Mistakes

Your Inner Critic also tries to help you avoid "mistakes." Like many of us, perhaps, you want to do your best at all times. So you listen to a self-critic who expects perfection. But perfection is like a unicorn: elusive because it doesn't exist. The Inner Critic tries anyway by pointing out your mistakes so you don't repeat them. This can take many forms. Consider Shawn's experience.

Shawn regularly spent time with a small, close-knit group of women friends. Every time they got together, her Inner Critic would be there, judging everything Shawn said: *Why did you say that? That makes you sound stupid.* Once, when she was really eager to make an important point in the conversation, she interrupted and blurted it out, but no one responded to her because another speaker was still talking. Shawn's Inner Critic went crazy! *Oh my God, you are so rude and loud! Why did you do that? They must think you are an attention seeker. And clearly, it was a dumb point anyway.* After that, Shawn was worried that she would talk too much or say dumb things, so she stayed quiet.

List the mistakes Shawn's Inner Critic was trying to correct.

_____

_____

_____

You may have come up with something like, "talking too much or "being impatient" or "thinking her point was important" or "assuming she has interesting things to say."

What pain do you think her Inner Critic was trying to help her avoid?

_____

_____

_____

Let's see how listening to her Inner Critic worked out.

Shawn's anxiety increased after that experience. She stopped joining the conversations with her friends. Now highly aware of the other women's behaviors toward her, she began imagining that the others were paying less and less attention to her. A headache developed, so she left the gathering early. Once home, she cried. She was drowning in thoughts about not fitting in; never having any "real" friends; even of dying alone and friendless.

Now it's your turn. Think back to the last "mistake" your Inner Critic warned you about. What was it?

_____

_____

_____

What pain was your Inner Critic trying to help you avoid?

_____

_____

_____

Consider that perceived mistakes and fears of pain are often not accurate. With that in mind, answer some more questions.

Did listening to your Inner Critic pacify the voice or make it louder?

_____

Did your response to the Inner Critic expand your life or make it smaller? Describe how.

_____

Overall, how did those corrections work out for you? What was the result?

_____

_____

_____

Toughening You Up So You Don't Get Hurt

Somewhere along the line, someone led you to believe that "tough love" is good for you. It's to be endured as a badge of honor. As a result, you likely not only rely on your Inner Critic to steer clear of mistakes and the discomfort they cause, you expect that inner voice to "knock sense" into you. It tends to attack when you didn't know about one of the many hurts and dangers that befall you in life.

Do you remember the story of Little Red Riding Hood? The folktale, and others like it, were first shared as cautionary tales to expose children to the dangers of the world in order to scare them into behaving. In the original French version of the story, Little Red Riding Hood, her grandmother, and the woodsman all pay a horrible price for her defiance when they are all eaten by the wolf. It teaches, "Don't be foolish and strike out on your own; it'll be your fault that you get yourself and others hurt. Or worse." Your Inner Critic is the result of cautionary lessons like this.

This is why you may justify the Inner Critic's scolding, devaluing, and place-putting by telling yourself that developing a thick skin, playing it safe, and not acknowledging disappointments or showing emotions are somehow healthy and useful strategies. Perhaps you have considered taking a risk, like asking the interesting person at the library out for coffee, only to have your Inner Critic pipe up with something like, *Who are you to think you could ask them out on a date? They are out of your league. They'll laugh in your face.* You may have dutifully agreed, thinking you dodged a bullet. But did you really?

Your Inner Critic loves simplicity. It divides everything into neat categories of right and wrong, good and bad, healthy and unhealthy, ugly and beautiful. It cuts to the chase in an effort to save you from having to think too much. In this way, it takes decision-making shortcuts. Through polarized thinking, the critic only offers two choices: yes or no. With clear-cut black-and-white binaries, the critic promises to easily eliminate mistakes and reach some idealized, faultless way of being in the world. In theory, this helps you make speedier, more confident decisions. Right?

Wrong. Life is infinitely complicated, messy, bountiful, and spectacular. It's colorful—actually an entire rainbow—not the pure black or white the Inner Critic craves. It's heartbreakingly limiting to only see two extremes. The Inner Critic makes absolute judgments that leave no room for the natural and nuanced ups and downs of life events, learning curves, personal growth, and the diversity of thought processes across humanity. By polarizing your identity, the Inner Critic is robbing you of appreciating your inherent worth beyond a narrow set of perceived successes or failures.

Consider a label like "lazy." It fails to account for the nuances of why you may sometimes struggle to take action. The Inner Critic casts a rigid, negative, presumed judgment of "lazy" based on one black or white factor like "no ambition." It doesn't consider the entire picture of why you may not be doing "enough." You may be experiencing poor health, burnout, or feelings of unworthiness. In essence, the critic merely assigns a mean and judgmental label without looking at context or function at all. It pigeonholes you and eventually stops you from living a full life of taking risks, feeding your curiosity, and opening to embrace new experiences.

Here are three journaling prompts that could help if you're struggling with polarized or black-and-white thinking. They ask you to notice those thought patterns, understand them with self-compassion, and consider more nuanced perspectives.

Exercise: Noticing the Nuances

Recall a time when your Inner Critic used polarized language with you. An example might be something like, *You messed up again! You're always messing up because you're so stupid.* What did it say to you?

_____

_____

_____

_____

Did its language and message make other things in that situation seem polarized or categorized in a black-and-white way? In the example, this would be either stupid or smart. Write down the polarity you see.

_____

_____

_____

Now zoom out and look at what the Inner Critic said through a wider lens. What other factors were at play in this situation? What details can you look at to illuminate the complexity of the situation?

Example: I didn't make the phone call in time because I fell asleep while the baby was finally sleeping after crying all night.

_____

_____

_____

_____

With this broader frame, do you gain a more nuanced perspective? Write down a new way to understand the situation and your behavior with more context and complexity. *Example: I am not stupid. I am exhausted and just wanted to close my eyes for five minutes.*

_____

_____

_____

_____

Staying Part, or Ahead, of the Group

We often evaluate ourselves to make sure we are fitting in with our larger social group (Deutsch and Gerard 1955; Festinger 1954). Some theorize this is left over from ancestral survival tactics to keep the group safe (Morgan and Laland 2012). Think of a school of fish: they tend to swim in a uniform pattern and any outliers swimming differently may draw attention and make the whole school vulnerable. This drive has evolved along with our species. Now, our assessment of conformity may have less to do with physical or literal safety, and more to do with keeping up with personal characteristics, such as attractiveness, intelligence, wealth, and success (Wills 1981). The explosion of social media has thrown this sort of social comparison in our faces, as it's a hyperspeed route to feeling crappy about ourselves. The reason? When we compare ourselves to others, it happens through a lens of *You're not enough.* That is the Inner Critic talking, by the way.

This isn't limited to social media engagement. Your Inner Critic is taking notes on how you are not measuring up in many aspects of your life. This is not new. The phrase "keeping up with the Joneses" first appeared over a century ago as the title of a newspaper comic strip about social climbing. Climbing is an apt metaphor for your fear of being left behind. The drive to be part of the group feels so important that you may overcompensate with a "more is better" perspective of group membership. Simply securing or maintaining a spot in the group may not be sufficient; it feels safer and more advantageous to strive to be ahead, to do more, to be better. If you aren't better, you aren't enough.

You don't have to look far in our hypercompetitive society to encounter all the messaging that insists who you are is not enough. You are barraged with advertisements to have the whitest smile, get your children into the best schools, have the most magical wedding, and so on. Because if it was good enough for your neighbor Dion's family, then you have to at least do that. Or more. The best is right. The best is desirable. The best is imperative. The best is good. If you aren't the best, you aren't good. And if you aren't good, you must be bad.

As a result, you expect your Inner Critic to alert you when you are not excelling, and you need to step up...which ends up being all the time. To *be better* is a never-ending task, like a tiger eating its tail. Because being better never ends. There is always room to be better, so you never arrive. Your Inner Critic is constantly reminding you that you need to do more. You aren't better. You aren't enough. As Theodore Roosevelt said, "Comparison is the thief of joy." Here are some examples of how comparison robs us of joy.

"I'm not as good a mom as _____."

"In my marriage, we don't talk or go on as many date nights as _____."

"I didn't make the team or get into that school like _____ did."

"They got that promotion! What's wrong with me? Why didn't I also get promoted?"

What are some comparisons you find yourself making? List three examples.

1. _____

2. _____

3. _____

There are more comparisons than we can name that amplify feelings of not being enough. When you transform your Inner Critic into a self-compassionate voice, you can look at yourself and say, *I am enough.* Even if there's a way you're not *doing* enough, you can compassionately, kindly, lovingly do whatever is needed.

Exercise: How You Measure Up

Look at how your self-critic's comments relate to personal characteristics, such as being attractive, intelligent, wealthy, successful—and more—relative to others. Record as many examples of what it says as you can.

_____

_____

_____

_____

Write about how you typically feel about yourself after spending time with a group of friends, coworkers, or family members.

_____

_____

_____

_____

Describe how you typically feel about yourself after hearing news about others' lives, like a close friend receiving a significant promotion or achieving some sort of accolade.

_____

_____

_____

_____

After you've earned a promotion or accolade, or achieved something significant, you may still compare your situation to others' successes. Write about the need to always be better. How does it make you feel?

_____

_____

_____

_____

After browsing social media and seeing what friends, coworkers, and influencers are doing, how do you typically feel about yourself? Describe any self-judgments arising from comparisons.

_____

_____

_____

_____

In any or all of these situations, you might assume that you don't actually have or do wonderful things. Comparison is sneaky. Say you just bought a new car, your partner just did something incredibly loving and thoughtful for you, or you just wrote a proposal that landed a big client. Yet, your critical inner voice questions it. Did someone else buy a better car? Is someone else's partner more attentive or attractive? Who got the bigger client? This can happen because your Inner Critic also compares your achievements to your own personal standards. Consider Claire's experience.

As an adult, Claire's relationship with her father was still challenging. Her lifelong pattern was to put her own needs aside to immediately take care of his needs whenever he asked for something. Despite this, Claire loved her father very much and emphasized how important it was to be respectful and kind. In therapy, she had been working on setting limits with him. But then her father was diagnosed with dementia.

One day, he called Claire repeatedly. Again and again, he interrupted a highly charged meeting with her supervisor. She shouted at him: "Stop calling me! You are being a pain in the ass, Dad. I'm done with you right now. Get someone else to help you with your dinner. I have important stuff going on here!"

Immediately after Claire hung up, she felt devastated. She had failed to live up to her own personal standards. Her self-critical voice told her: *You're a horrible and selfish person for not giving Dad the patience and kindness that he needs. Maybe Dad is right that I'm not worth caring about.* She couldn't function at work, didn't eat for several days, and even contemplated suicide. Her critic was adamant that not living up to her own standards was completely unacceptable.

What do you think? If Claire were your friend, would you think she was a selfish, awful human being, unworthy of affection? It can feel deeply shameful when we aren't able to meet the standards we hold for ourselves. Often, we consider this question about another person and think, *It's not very shameful at all. None of us is perfect!* But do you extend this same grace to yourself? Let's look at the shame you feel when you aren't able to meet the standards you hold for yourself.

Exercise: Personal Standards

When the Inner Critic speaks, it often communicates with mandates. It uses words like "have to" and "should," which indicate its unreasonably high expectations and standards. Let's look at the mandates your critical inner voice uses.

What do you *have to* do or be? These are things you think you *have to* do, and do perfectly. Here are two examples: *I must make dinner from scratch every night for my family. I have to come into the office early and stay later than everyone else to be seen as competent at my job.*

_____

_____

_____

_____

_____

Consider your *shoulds*, the things you think you always *should* or *shouldn't* do and be. For example, *I should be happy all the time and I shouldn't complain*. Write what your Inner Critic says to you.

I should: _____

_____

_____

_____

I shouldn't: _____

_____

_____

_____

Maintaining Your Motivation

You may have been led to believe that harsh, critical language compels a person to act or change. But this severe pressure is not motivating at all. While you want a voice to encourage you, push you forward, foster a sense of confidence, and increase your ability to get things done, the Inner Critic actually keeps you stuck. It doesn't truly motivate anyone. Rather, it causes pain and suffering before you can rally to get back up and get going.

Think of a baby learning to walk. When that baby falls, which they inevitably will, do we say, "You stupid baby, what is wrong with you? You can do better, stop falling, get up and walk!"? The very thought of saying that can make us feel ill. Consider that even if the baby gets up and walks, what was the cost? That harsh language will harm their sense of self-worth and damage feelings of security, confidence, and agency. Yet that is the very same harsh language we use on ourselves.

What *does* motivate are words of encouragement. If, after tumbling, the baby heard, "Okay, good job. I'm so proud of you. You are walking. Look at you, I bet you can get up again and walk some more!" how might the baby feel? Pretty darn ready to get up and walk again. That is encouragement at work, actually being motivating.

The reason you continue to listen to your critic is because the *expected* functions it serves sound helpful and productive at first pass. You think the Inner Critic is an assistant, pointing things out to you. It's helpful to anticipate when something might stir unwelcome emotions, be notified when you might make mistakes, keep tabs on where you want to be socially, and motivate you to stay on task, right?

Yet the most impactful feature of these feedback sessions with the critic isn't its observations or "helpful" tips—it's how terribly the Inner Critic *tears you down*. Think of the nasty names it calls you. If it were a real-life assistant, would you let them talk to you that way? No. So why do you let *you* talk to you that way?

The Critic's Actual Function: Punishment

We have been sharing what people commonly *expect* the function of the critic to be rather than what the function of the critic *turns out* to be. To do this, consider the word *function*. Often, it's used casually to indicate the purpose or action that something accomplishes. However, what we actually mean is its expected outcome—how we desire something to work for us. We confuse what we *hope* the voice of the critic might do for us (problem solve, offer guidance, provide data for comparison, or make us feel happier) for how things *actually* end up.

Your high expectations for your Inner Critic to do right by you and keep you safe are what keep it in the driver's seat. While this driver seems like they are on top of things, they are taking you in a direction away from where you want to go. Punishment is the actual function of the critical inner voice.

The Inner Critic as encouraging motivator turns out to be a brutal punisher more times than not. It lashes out, saying nasty things and bossing you around. It calls you "stupid" or "incompetent." Rather than making you feel confident, the Inner Critic makes you feel just the opposite.

It's easy to believe that this critical inner voice that is calling you names is the only voice you have. But you are not, in fact, just your Inner Critic. You are so much more, but when you talk to yourself this way, it's hard to remember your capacity to also be kind and loving and tender toward yourself. Just as kind and tender and loving as you would be toward that baby. Just as that baby got right back up and continued walking when spoken to gently, so can you.

Who wouldn't learn to hate themselves over time when they're listening to the critic catalog all the times and ways they've made mistakes, done the wrong thing, disappointed themselves, broken the "rules," been vulnerable…and so much else? To begin gaining an objective view of your punishing Inner Critic, we'll explore the names it calls you.

Exercise: The Names You Call Yourself

You likely have names you call yourself—names you would never call another human being you cared about. They may seem too embarrassing or shameful to pluck out of your mind and actually write down here on the page. Well, when you bring all those hurtful names out from the dark place within you and into the light, you begin to diminish the painful hold they have on you. Really. It's okay. We hope you might trust us a little bit by this point. Claire will go first. You are not alone. We promise.

Claire used to call herself a "fat, disgusting, stupid, f'ing cow." She'd mumble it to herself, in an almost compulsive, repetitive way whenever she was really upset—which was a lot of the time.

What are hurtful names you call yourself? Take a deep breath and write them down.

_____

_____

_____

_____

Are there other really awful, painful, punishing things you tell yourself ? Some things we've heard from clients, or that have been said by one of us, include:

I talk too much. I'm so annoying.

I can't believe I just said that. They must think I'm such an idiot!

Oh my god! Shut it! Stop being a crybaby and get over yourself!

Write down as many of your self-punishing statements as you can.

_____

_____

_____

_____

Time for a check in: How are you feeling? That may have been a pretty rough exercise. Here's the thing. Before you start feeling frustrated with us, stirring things up and causing you to feel worse, please remember that you are already saying these things to yourself. Probably daily. Like many of us, maybe hourly. This workbook is not *creating* new pain for you, it is shining a flashlight on pain that you already carry. Remember, the initial steps toward cultivating self-compassion to soothe your Inner Critic and make its voice less insistent ask you to increase awareness of what is happening. That is what we are doing now.

Exercise: Listening to Your Self-Compassionate Voice

Put your hand on your heart, breathe in, and sit with how uncomfortable—how painful—this feels right now. Can you simply *be* without fighting? Without judging? Without judging yourself? Can you sit with the pain in the service of this step toward a kinder way of being and a life that feels richer and more meaningful? Write about your experience.

_____

_____

_____

_____

_____

_____

Let's look at how the Inner Critic's voice can prevent you from doing things that are important to you. Read through Rohan's story and then reflect on it.

During a recent cross-country race, Rohan was expected to finish in the top three, but found himself consistently behind the front-runners. He was not able to rally for a top finish, and in fact, finished in fifth place among a field of ten runners. By the time he reached the finish line, his self-critical voice was so strong that he skipped the team's post-race celebration and instead headed straight home to bed, where he stayed for the next three days.

Write down what you imagine Rohan's Inner Critic was saying during the race and afterward.

_____

_____

_____

_____

Recall the distinction between *expected* versus *actual* function and consider how these critical thoughts actually affected Rohan. What purpose did these thoughts actually serve? Describe the function of Rohan's self-critical talk.

_____

_____

_____

_____

You may have observed that Rohan's self-talk ultimately wasn't able to get him to the front of the pack. And it kept him from enjoying finishing the race or celebrating the achievements of all the runners, including his own respectable fifth place. It also kept him in bed for a long time afterward, stewing over what happened to him and his perceived failure, shame, and suffering.

When you think about the Inner Critic's actual function versus the ways you think, or hope, it'll work for you, it becomes apparent that the actual function of the Inner Critic is to make you feel really terrible. This was certainly the case for Rohan.

Exercise: Consequences of Listening to the Inner Critic's Voice

Can you remember a time when your critical voice left you feeling like you wanted to skip the celebration, so to speak, and just go to bed? Think back to a recent situation when your Inner Critic's messages didn't fulfill their intended function. Write down what your critical voice was telling you at that time.

_____

_____

_____

Now consider the outcome that critical voice was hoping to achieve. Write down its intentions.

_____

_____

_____

What were the actual consequences of listening to the self-critic? In other words, what ended up happening? Describe both the short-term and long-term effects.

_____

_____

_____

_____

_____

_____

_____

The Coach: Your Productive Inner Voice

You may be thinking, *Hey! Sometimes an inner voice has helped me! One time it reminded me that it was really important to stay a little late at work. I was finishing up a project and, even though I was tired, I stayed and pushed through. My boss noticed and I got a promotion.* That's great. It's true, sometimes your inner voice can be productive and helpful.

But guess what? That's not your Inner Critic speaking. That's a different voice, which we'll define for you in a moment. The Inner Critic is mean, degrading, harsh, and judgmental. It leaves you feeling worse off about yourself, not better. So if you have a value, like doing well at work, the Inner Critic might say, *Sure, stay late to finish that project. But it won't make a difference because you're not smart enough to get it done right anyway.* That is the Inner Critic speaking.

On the other hand, the voice you hear that encourages, supports, and guides you—without criticism—is what we call *The Coach*. Its messages are effective, helpful, and motivating. The standards it holds us up to come from our values (which you'll learn about in chapter 6), not from comparisons to others. Think of The Coach as productive—reminding you of what's important and gently moving you in that direction. The Inner Critic tells you all the reasons you can't get there.

You are not working through this book because The Coach is the only voice guiding you. So let's continue to distinguish between the Inner Critic and The Coach. Then you'll learn to turn down the volume on the Inner Critic's voice so you can hear The Coach more clearly. As you keep working with your coach, it'll take some time, but you can pivot from being driven by your critical voice to being led and helped by your coach. By consistently practicing the skills in this book, it'll become easier.

Melissa is a young woman struggling with feelings of inadequacy and self-doubt. After recently graduating with an advanced degree from a prestigious university, she has been looking for a job. But no offers have come, as she had expected they would. She confided to a friend that, "I'm just not good enough. I had the worst interview, they thought I was totally unprepared, and I sounded like an idiot. I didn't know what I was doing." Melissa berated herself for not living up to the expectations that she set for herself. The narrative became wholly unproductive.

But then Melissa caught herself. She realized it was time for The Coach. She wanted help identifying what she needed to do differently to interview more effectively. Melissa listed ways in which she felt uncertain and unskilled. She then wrote down ways in which she could become more informed and practice interpersonal skills to help her feel more at ease in the interview process. By bringing in The Coach, Melissa was able to gain perspective and create a plan to improve her interview skills while building confidence and speaking to her expertise.

To be clear, The Coach is not about lying to ourselves. It is about being honest with ourselves and holding ourselves accountable. What is encouraging about being accountable is that we have an opportunity to change our behavior without harsh punishment. In this next exercise, you have the chance to choose coach over critic.

Exercise: Choose the Voice You Listen To

Describe a situation that brings up pain for you.

_____

_____

_____

_____

What do you wish could be different about that situation?

_____

_____

_____

What is the Inner Critic saying in response?

_____

_____

_____

How do you feel after listening to those messages? Describe how it is causing more pain and suffering.

_____

_____

_____

What is The Coach saying? Is it offering any productive alternatives?

_____

_____

_____

How do you feel after listening to The Coach?

_____

_____

_____

You have a choice. Would you rather feel negative about yourself after listening to the Inner Critic? Or would you like to feel positive about yourself after listening to The Coach? Write about the differences between the two and make a choice.

_____

_____

_____

_____

_____

What does the Inner Critic really do for you? Hopefully, in working through the exercises in this chapter, you've realized that the voice of the Inner Critic can leave you feeling bad about yourself, demotivated, and even demoralized—a far cry from its intention. The more you cultivate the ability to recognize your self-critic's actual function, as well as its intended function, the more able you'll be to clear the way for your inner, helpful, kind coach to speak instead.

As you read on, we'll guide you through ways self-compassion can turn the Inner Critic into the The Coach. In the next chapter, we emphasize how important it is to quiet your inner critical voice and develop the voice of your inner coach. Because that sneaky critic is not just going to go away all by itself.

CHAPTER 3

The Critic's Role in Your Cycle of Distress

Until now, you've had high expectations that your Inner Critic will guide you to a better, safer version of yourself. But it does far more harm than good. Living with the Inner Critic goes beyond the agony of listening to negative self-talk all the time; it also has significant costs. Your Inner Critic may rob your life of joy and meaning. It can lead to patterns of distress and pain that cycle downward into debilitating mental health issues. Our hope is that, as you read through this section, you will decide that the costs are too great. Then you will say "Yes!" to practicing self-compassion as an antidote.

As we mentioned, both "positive" and "negative" emotions are neither good nor bad; they are simply giving you data. In this chapter, we highlight what may be happening as you let the Inner Critic dominate and allow it to call the shots. A passive stance can lead to very negative consequences. Specifically, when you believe that avoiding negative emotions is useful and healthy, and you listen to the Inner Critic's "protective" attempts, you are perpetuating a cycle of self-critical behavior that can lead to depression, anxiety, social isolation, and shame. In this chapter, we'll dive into that cycle, its effects, and how you can begin to interrupt it.

Habitually Distressed

All of us feel unpleasant emotions throughout the course of our lives. The experience of emotional discomfort and pain, in and of itself, is not an indication of an active critical inner voice. When a habitual cycle of self-critical thoughts causes us pain, and we react to that emotional pain with more critical thoughts, that is when emotional suffering becomes frequent and unbearable. Constantly stuck in a cycle of self-critical thoughts, and inevitably painful emotions, only elicits more attempts to get rid of those distressing feelings. After all, who wants to feel miserable about themselves all the time? Have you noticed that the more you try to alleviate the feelings you don't want, the more you seem to have them? Yup, it happens to us too.

There's a paradox here. Trying harder to "fix" your feelings actually causes you to spend more and more time with them. You end up feeling cruddy for longer. So you spend more and more time trying to fix how awful you feel, and then spend yet more time focused on those feelings. Lather. Rinse. Repeat. Voila—there's your cycle.

Maybe you, like us, have been in this self-critical cycle so often, and for so long, that you fail to notice how harshly you are evaluating yourself. You may forget that you are criticizing yourself at all because self-criticism is your primary approach to thinking about yourself. Or you fail to recognize how uncomfortable and distressed you are feeling until one day, just how awful you feel suddenly catches up with you.

To gauge how you're feeling as a result of how you're treating yourself, look at your behavioral patterns. This is an act of self-compassion. The best way to look at patterns is to observe and track yourself over the next two weeks. Two weeks might seem like a big commitment, especially if you have a lot on your plate, but you can quickly log your feelings daily for five to ten minutes. We recommend that you track as you continue to engage the rest of the workbook. If that feels overwhelming, come back to this exercise when you're ready to commit to doing it. We've provided a filled-out sample worksheet, as well as one blank version. Of course, to do the full two weeks of practice, you'll need additional copies of this worksheet. Visit http://www .newharbinger.com/54292 to download and print those. Here's how Lee filled out the worksheet one day.

Sample Exercise: Tracking How You Feel

Situation: At a party, I told a joke to my friends. No one laughed. Then after leaving the party, I cried alone at home.

What I wanted to happen: I wanted to be heard. I wanted to not feel the pain of embarrassment.

What my Inner Critic said: At the party, it said, *You aren't funny, you are a loser who no one likes.* At home it said, *You're an immature baby. Grow up. You're pitiful.*

How I felt: At the party, I felt ashamed, embarrassed, sad, and mad at myself. At home afterward, I felt hopeless.

What I did: At the party, I sat alone in the other room and left the party early. I cried all the way home. Once home, I drank three shots of tequila.

How that worked for me: I still feel embarrassed. I was not heard. I missed out on celebrating Anna and Gina's engagement. I spent the rest of the night feeling lonely, mad at myself for leaving, and embarrassed about acting like a baby. I felt sick and eventually passed out on the sofa. My roommate is now mad because they couldn't wake me up and they were worried.

Intensity of feelings on a scale of 1 to 10: 8 when it happened; 9 in the other room; 7 the next morning.

Duration of feelings: Three days.

Here's the worksheet you can fill out, ongoing, to track your experience.

Exercise: Tracking How You Feel

Situation: _____

_____

_____

What I wanted to happen: _____

_____

_____

What my Inner Critic said: _____

_____

_____

How I felt: _____

_____

What I did: _____

_____

How that worked for me: _____

_____

Intensity of feelings on a scale of 1 to 10: _____

Duration of feelings: _____

_____

This may seem like a lot. And it is. But what is the alternative? To keep doing what you're doing? That's what a cycle is. By asking you to track your self-critical voice and its effects, our intent is to help you break old cycles that don't work for you. We hope you are invested in the journey and will give yourself this self-care gift.

Exercise: Reflect on Your Self-Critical Situations

After you've completed the tracking exercise for two weeks, take a look at your observations altogether. See if you can notice any trends.

What were you hoping would happen or change?

_____

_____

_____

_____

List the feelings that came up for you during the two-week period.

_____

_____

_____

_____

How did you react to those thoughts and feelings? What did you do?

_____

_____

_____

_____

How much pain were you in, and for how long?

_____

_____

Identifying Functions

Next, we'll look at the expected and actual functions of the Inner Critic that you learned in chapter 2. Gather your logs from the last two weeks. For each situation, write down the expected function of the Inner Critic. Here are some of the functions we discussed in chapter 2, but there are others, so write down what's true for you. Your Inner Critic may hope to:

- keep you safe from unwanted emotions

- prevent you from making mistakes

- toughen you up to keep you from getting hurt

- simplify decisions

- keep you part, or ahead, of the group

- maintain motivation to stay on task

Do any specific types and functions of self-critical thoughts show up more than others? Write down any themes or patterns that emerge across the experiences you tracked.

_____

_____

_____

_____

If you are struggling to name the pattern of distress you may be experiencing, you're not alone. This can be challenging to do, so we're devoting the rest of this chapter to it. It's very common that, when you are in a pattern of distress, you are unaware of it. The idea that your distress has become a "pattern" can lead you to believe that what you're feeling is no big deal, something you deserve, and simply needs to be endured. Just as you are coming to see that the Inner Critic has duped you into believing it's looking out for your best interests, you can see that it is keeping you stuck in an unworkable cycle of distress.

Patterns of Distress

Self-critical cycles leave you suffering from the critic's harsh voice *and* the fallout of your reactions to it. Over time, you develop habitual ways of coping to wrangle that ongoing cycle of suffering. These coping tendencies are a last-ditch effort to avoid emotional pain. Because they might avoid the sting of unpleasant feelings in the moment, you likely use them again and again. This is how you have developed a habitual pattern of critical reactions. Yet, coping-by-avoidance patterns often add even more suffering in the long run and are unhelpful. This is what the pattern of habitual reactions looks like.

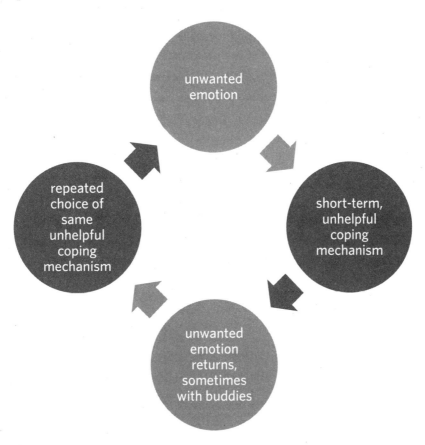

While every person's suffering is unique and specific to their situation, we often cope with suffering in similar ways. In this workbook, we organized those ways of coping into three common patterns: *withdrawal into sadness and depression, anxious worry,* and *shameful avoidance.*

In their most extreme forms, depression and anxiety can reach clinically significant levels, including diagnosable disorders. Discussing diagnosis and treatment goes beyond what we can offer in this workbook. If you need support for depression, anxiety, or any clinical concerns, we encourage you to seek the help of a mental health professional. Doing so can be deeply beneficial, even lifesaving. You deserve to receive that support.

Now let's explore times you've fallen into these patterns after encounters with your Inner Critic. There may be overlap between descriptions. What form of distress do you most recognize in yourself?

Withdrawal into Sadness and Depression

Your Inner Critic may keep you stuck: feeling blue and down, at times melancholy, helpless, or even hopeless. These feelings can prevent you from seeking vitality, joy, and purpose—even when you are still able to attend to your tasks throughout the day. Sadness may elicit withdrawal, disengagement, and lack of interest as you just go through the motions.

Depression, however, is an extreme expression of these feelings that persists for a long period of time. You might pull back from life so much that you begin to question the point of doing things, having relationships, or even existing. If you think you are experiencing depression, please seek professional help.

When your Inner Critic shows up, do you experience any feelings of melancholy or sadness? Describe what you feel in your body and some of the behaviors you might engage in.

_____

_____

_____

_____

Anxious Worry

As with depression, severe anxiety interferes with daily living. If your anxiety is so pronounced that you are unable to perform day-to-day tasks, please seek professional help. It's also true that most of us experience anxiety from time to time. It is part of the familiar fight, flight, freeze response to stress and perceived threat. Recall chapter 1, where we discussed how your body and mind evolved to mobilize your defenses. They keep you safe and alive, teaching you to avoid places and situations that are threatening. This response system can become problematic when it *over* responds, classifying even mundane interactions with others and the world as dangerous. This system can even respond to internal experiences—such as uncomfortable thoughts, emotions, memories, and images—as "threats."

Worry is the behavior of excessively thinking about future threats to oneself, others, or the world. This negative forecasting is extreme, distracting, and often all-consuming. Worry and anxiety can feel like unpleasant physical sensations and excessive feelings of uneasiness or fear. It can also bring about a sense of dread or doom. If anxious worry is a coping pattern for you, you likely also experience avoidance, guardedness, fear, and rumination about the future.

When your Inner Critic shows up, do you experience any of these signs of anxiety and worry? Describe what you feel in your body and some of the behaviors you engage in when experiencing these feelings.

_____

_____

_____

_____

Shameful Avoidance

You may believe that you have acted in a foolish, inept, or disgraceful way and may therefore attempt to minimize or hide your actions, thoughts, or feelings from others. Our feelings of shame cause us to close down around ourselves, to disengage and drop connection from activities and people we care about. Brené Brown (2021) describes shame as "…the intensely painful feeling or experience of believing that we are flawed and therefore unworthy of love, belonging, and connection." If shameful avoidance is a familiar coping pattern, you likely experience fear, disconnection, secrecy, and critical self-judgment.

When your Inner Critic shows up, do you experience feelings of shame? Describe what you feel in your body and some of the behaviors you might engage when you experience these feelings.

_____

_____

_____

_____

Exercise: Naming Your Patterns of Distress

Now that you have explored three common patterns of coping with your harsh Inner Critic, let's return to the Tracking How You Feel worksheets you completed. Review them, one at a time, and write down the pattern of distress—withdrawal into sadness, anxious worry, or shameful avoidance—that best characterizes your emotional responses and the actions that followed each situation. Some situations may have resulted in more than one pattern. If no pattern fits, add your own.

Which pattern of distress shows up most often for you? Circle one.

Withdrawal into sadness and depression

Anxious worry

Shameful avoidance

Do different situations, or functions of the Inner Critic, result in different distress responses? Write each type of situation and describe the distress response you experience.

_____

_____

_____

_____

Overall, does the voice of your Inner Critic leave you feeling okay? Or not so okay?

_____

_____

_____

_____

Feeling Unworthy of Love and Connection

Looking back on your tracking worksheets, how often did shame come up? It likely came up at least once, and perhaps in all cases. That's because shame is insidious and the most prevalent pattern we see in our clients. So we'll investigate this emotion further and share how you can decrease its intensity.

Shame is an integral part of a cycle of distress, so much so that you may not be aware of how often you experience it. It may be so perpetual that you are used to how it feels and don't even recognize that you are living with it.

Feelings of shame can cause you to close down around yourself, disengage, and drop connection from activities and people you care about. More often than not, shame leads to social isolation as your pain and suffering reinforces your sense of unworthiness. This is why shame, and the disconnection from others it causes, can be the most painful and destructive part of our self-critical cycle.

Relationships are integral to well-being. We are social beings. Connecting with, being seen by, caring for, and loving other humans is central to how we can be in the world when we are thriving. This cannot be understated! Relationships give our lives meaning. They are a large part of what moves us in the direction of what we value and what enriches us. Reducing shame, and its disconnection and isolation, can be a ticket out of the self-critical cycle. You will learn ways to improve your connection to others in chapter 5.

In her book *The Gifts of Imperfection*, Brené Brown (2010) identifies three conditions that sustain shame: secrecy, silence, and judgment. She also identifies three ways to practice worthiness, which decreases shame: courage, compassion, and connection. Let's try an exercise to explore the ways you may be harboring shame and how to lessen it.

Exercise: Living with Shame

We invite you to notice yourself when you are living with shame. Write down three things that cause you to experience shame.

1. _____

2. _____

3. _____

Describe what happens when you keep shame a *secret*.

_____

_____

_____

_____

Think about what happens when you stay *silent*. When you struggle to talk about what causes you shame, what tends to happen to the feeling?

_____

_____

_____

Write about what happens when you *judge* your shame.

_____

_____

_____

_____

_____

Now imagine what it would be like to muster the courage to connect with another person to speak about your shame. Write down what needs to happen for you to find this *courage*.

_____

_____

_____

_____

_____

What would have to happen for you to *connect* with another person and open up about these feelings?

_____

_____

_____

_____

_____

When you tracked your self-critical thinking on your worksheets, it may have become apparent that your Inner Critic, and the shame it brings, can really get in the way of doing what matters to you. It encourages you to play it safe and live small, so you don't get hurt by feelings like embarrassment, or anyone's judgments, or activating painful rules and self-stories.

Exercise: Listening to Your Self-Compassionate Voice

Before we go further, let's check in. Put one or both hands on your heart, breathe in, and sit with any discomfort or other unwanted emotions. Can you just *be* without fighting it? Without judging it? Without judging yourself? Can you sit with this pain in the service of taking steps toward a kinder way of being—toward a life that feels richer and more meaningful? Write about what you experience.

_____

_____

_____

_____

_____

Breaking the Cycle

You may be wondering: *Do I have the courage it takes to* quiet *the Inner Critic? How do I begin to be compassionate with this voice and myself? I'm not sure….* We get it! Even after you have a sense of how painful the Inner Critic is and how it might be holding you back, you might be daunted by the prospect of making peace with it and changing your behavior. After all, for all the reasons it came into being, it's understandable to think you might not be able to break away from it.

You have a choice: continue doing what you have been doing and suffering how you have been suffering. Or work to change those behaviors. This is an opportunity to do something different. The hardest part of the workbook is behind you. Now, the exciting, transformative, promising work is ahead.

Your *willingness* will help you the most—staying open to whatever feelings come up. Negative or positive, pleasant or painful, you can continue to move toward what you value and what makes life meaningful. Willingness allows you to stay focused on what's important rather than becoming distracted by trying to make painful feelings go away. We have every confidence that you will continue bringing willingness to this work going forward. We'll help you hone the self-compassion and kindness toward yourself that will help you along the path.

Exercise: Envisioning a Different Way

Please read through these instructions before beginning the next exercise. You can also access a recorded version of this exercise at http://www.newharbinger.com/54292. Find a quiet spot where you will not be interrupted for five to ten minutes. Close your eyes or gently hold your gaze in front of you.

If you feel comfortable, put your hands over your heart and begin by taking five slow, deep breaths. Be aware of your breath going in through your nose and out through your mouth. Notice the rise and fall of your chest with each breath.

With your eyes still closed or focused, expand your awareness to recall a time when your Inner Critic spoke to you in a way that caused you suffering.

What did it say?

Notice the tone of voice it uses. Where do you feel its message in your body? What are those sensations like? See if you can name any tingling, heat, tension, and so on. Recall how your Inner Critic's harshness affected the moments that followed.

How did it affect the next day?

Were there other effects that took longer to unfold?

If your mind starts to wander during this exercise, as it inevitably will, gently bring yourself back to that moment of pain through your breath and your sense of touch.

Take another breath, allowing that experience to fade. Let this take as long as it takes.

Now, we invite you to offer yourself another way.

Envision what it would look and feel like to be kinder to yourself. There are no steps yet. There are no wrong answers, no wrong ways. We want you to get a sense of what being kinder to yourself looks and feels like.

Where do you feel kindness in your body?

What are those sensations? See if you can name any tingling, warmth, relaxation, and so on.

How might those feelings affect the next few moments of your life? The next few days?

Bring your awareness back to your breath. Widen your attention, taking in the sounds around you, feeling your body in the seat, and gently opening your eyes. When you feel ready, write about what you just experienced.

_____

_____

_____

_____

_____

_____

_____

What you just did is a process of envisioning. Imagining where you would like to be, and what that would be like—in the process of life change—has been shown to be helpful (D'Argembeau et al. 2010; Gooding 2004; Sheldon and Lyubomirsky 2006). Ultimately, envisioning how you want your life to be is a way to create the steps to get there and anticipate how it will feel. This can guide you in the course of behavior change. It's most effective, of course, when you combine consistency with practice.

The painful effects of the Inner Critic are important to become aware of in order to change them. Notice what the Inner Critic drives you to do, as you disconnect or isolate from the very activities and people you want to engage. It makes you feel bad about yourself and perpetuates a cycle of negative self-regard, often leading even more negative self-talk.

But when you clarify what is important to you, what truly matters to you, and use self-compassion and willingness to stay connected, even if your Inner Critic speaks, you can adjust to stay aligned with meaning and vitality. You'll practice making peace with your Inner Critic along the way.

CHAPTER 4

Self-Compassion Can Quiet the Critic

Self-compassion is the practice of treating yourself with kind, loving, gentle understanding. But what does that actually look like? Is it as simple as talking kindly to yourself when the Inner Critic gets loud? In this chapter, we'll explore what self-compassion is and what it is not, briefly touching on common misconceptions. We'll guide you to identify what it looks and feels like, and how to use it when interrupting the cycles of your Inner Critic and your particular patterns of distress. By the end of this chapter, you'll know how to tap into the voice of your coach to support a regular self-compassion practice.

Exercise: What Do You Think Self-Compassion Is?

Put this book down. Go do something for yourself, whatever that thing happens to be. Give yourself at least ten minutes. Then write what you did and reflect on why you chose that activity.

_____

_____

_____

_____

When Shawn did this exercise, she got up from the book, folded a load of laundry, put it away, and came back to the book. Was that self-compassion? *Hmmm.* This is where it gets tricky. The answer is—it depends.

We can find clues in Shawn's reasoning. One thinking pattern goes like this: *If I don't get this laundry put away, it just proves that I'm lazy and messy and can't ever get things done. So if I do this now, maybe I won't be those things.*

Another thinking pattern sounds like this: *I can spend a few moments now to finish this, and my space will be just a bit tidier and more peaceful.*

Which one feels like compassion to you? _____

Of course, it may have been that your response was a third choice: neither of these choices feels very self-compassionate to you. After all, is doing a chore really what self-compassion is about?

Was your reasoning for choosing your activity an expression of self-compassion? Why or why not?

_____

_____

_____

_____

_____

For Shawn, the activity wasn't about the laundry at all. It was about the function that putting the laundry away served, as knowing that putting it away would give her a degree of relaxation and peace of mind she couldn't have in a messy space. It also offered an opportunity to mindfully focus on something calming. Doesn't that sound like extending kindness to herself?

We offer this specific example to emphasize the point that self-compassion does not necessarily mean grand gestures, like long meditations. Or exclusively comforting things, like bubble baths. Self-compassion is about extending quiet kindness to yourself. Even, and perhaps *especially*, when choosing quiet kindness seems difficult.

Understanding Compassion

To best understand self-compassion, it is helpful to first understand compassion itself. It combines three conditions: *kindness, a sense of common humanity,* and *mindfulness.* Together, they create awareness of another's suffering and a desire to alleviate it (Neff and Germer 2013). You have likely experienced compassion for someone else at some time or another, and you can use this as a starting point to foster compassion for yourself.

Exercise: Compassion for Others

Think of a time you encountered someone in emotional pain and extended compassion toward them. Reflect on that experience as you answer the following questions.

What was the source of this person's pain?

_____

_____

What did you do in response?

_____

_____

What did you feel when you realized they were in pain?

_____

_____

How did the encounter end? Describe what happened.

_____

_____

_____

Did your relationship with this person, feelings about them, regard for them, or your connection with them change? If so, in what way?

_____

_____

_____

Was offering compassion easy or difficult for you? Describe any instincts or challenges you experienced.

_____

_____

_____

We suspect you're good at caring about what a loved one is going through and treating them gently. Maybe you picked up this book because while you're thoughtful and caring with others, you're not so good at giving the same attention to yourself. Good news: your impulse to help others in distress can be turned toward yourself. The rest of this book offers ways to do that.

Let's explore the three conditions of compassion some more. *Kindness, a sense of common humanity,* and *mindfulness* come together to form compassion that can be directed toward others and yourself.

Kindness

The Dalai Lama says, "Be kind whenever possible. It is always possible." Kindness is benevolence, caring, and genuine generosity toward others as well as ourselves. An important distinction needs to be made between kindness and "niceness." To be *nice* is to be agreeable and acquiescing. It refers to pleasing others and being polite. Being nice to others all too often leads us to disregard our own needs, causing resentment and self-judgment. Do you know the difference? This exercise will help clarify it.

Exercise: Kind or Nice?

Think of a recent time you acted with *niceness*; that is, you were agreeable, acquiescent, polite. Hold that experience in mind as you answer the following questions.

How did you demonstrate those characteristics? What actions did you take and what words did you say?

_____

_____

_____

_____

How did those responses feel, emotionally and in your body?

_____

_____

Now think of a recent time you acted with *kindness*; that is with benevolence, care, generosity. Again, consider what that experience was like as you reflect on these questions.

How did you demonstrate those characteristics with actions and words? What did you do or say?

_____

_____

_____

How did these responses feel, emotionally and in your body?

_____

_____

Can you see a difference between the two situations? Maybe the outcome was different, or you felt better in one situation than the other. Write what you observe, now that you know about the distinction between being kind and being nice.

_____

_____

_____

_____

_____

_____

Common Humanity

Even though being aware of our common humanity may sound complicated or daunting, what it means is pretty straightforward. We all understand that emotional pain happens to everyone. Humans suffer in common ways, so we are not alone in the depths of our pain. However, you may not have considered this when navigating your own suffering. Let's explore awareness of our common humanity together.

Exercise: Shared Human Experience

Think of an experience that caused painful feelings. It could be the relentlessly harsh words of your Inner Critic, the loss of a loved one, or a significant disappointment, for example. Consider what that felt like as you answer the following questions.

Write down the feelings you experienced.

_____

_____

Did you feel alone or cut off from other people because of this experience and your feelings about it?

_____

_____

Now imagine that someone in the world, among almost 8 billion people, had the same experience and felt the same way as you. The same feelings, the same thoughts, and the same disconnection and loneliness.

How does it feel to know that a person out there is feeling the same as you? Check in with yourself and write what you notice.

_____

_____

If you could talk to this person, what would you ask them?

_____

_____

If you could talk to this person, what might you learn from their experience?

_____

_____

If you could talk to this person, what would you tell them about your experience?

_____

_____

If you could talk to this person, what might they learn from you about their experience?

_____

_____

Mindfulness

You have likely heard of mindfulness before. It's a skill that involves "paying attention in a particular way: on purpose, in the present moment, and nonjudgmentally" (Kabat-Zinn 1994). Evidence shows that mindfulness is related to lower levels of depression and anxiety, can lead to better sleep, and can help with emotion regulation. It has been shown to help patients with chronic pain and other physical disorders navigate their distress more effectively. Mindfulness offers a way of cultivating effective behaviors in the present moment. Many therapeutic practices now incorporate mindfulness into healing strategies, and apps like Headspace and Calm have gained popularity. We live in stressful times, so by slowing down and connecting with the present moment before we act, we can learn how to navigate distress.

Because mindfulness is a key component of compassion, it may be helpful to consider that when we practice compassion using mindfulness, we are expanding our hearts.

Perhaps you have tried some mindfulness practices? Let's do a basic one here. Because mindful awareness is a key component to self-compassion practice, we'll be doing many more mindfulness exercises throughout the rest of this workbook.

Exercise: Take a Minute to Be Mindful

Here are three of our favorite one-minute mindful awareness exercises. For each, time yourself for one minute as you observe your experience using all five senses. Then, respond to the following prompts. Be aware of judgment when it arises (and it will!), meet it with kindness, and return to observation. Judgment may sound like: *It's embarrassing that my garbage smells, how did I let it get that bad? Ugh, I hate that song. I'm not doing this exercise right, it's stupid.* Once you get the hang of the exercise, feel free to make up some mindful activities of your own.

Activity 1: Steep a Cup of Tea

What does it feel like? _____

_____

What are you seeing? _____

_____

What smells are you aware of? _____

_____

What does it sound like? _____

_____

Do you notice any taste? _____

_____

What judgments come up? _____

_____

Activity 2: Wash Dishes by Hand

What does it feel like? _____

_____

What are you seeing? _____

_____

What smells are you aware of? _____

_____

What does it sound like? _____

_____

Do you notice any taste? _____

_____

What judgments come up? _____

_____

Activity 3: Be Right Where You Are, at This Moment

What does it feel like? _____

_____

What are you seeing? _____

_____

What smells are you aware of? _____

_____

What does it sound like? _____

_____

Do you notice any taste? _____

_____

What judgments come up? _____

_____

When you combine nonjudgmental awareness of your world, those in it, and yourself with kindness and a sense of our common human experience, you are practicing compassion. The practice of self-compassion is therefore to mindfully extend kindness to yourself and reinforce your sense of universal connection with others. We are all fallible, with the same kinds of thoughts, feelings, behaviors, and Inner Critics. You can recognize that you also deserve your own kindness. That sounds simple…and yet? It's not so easy to actually do.

Embracing Self-Compassion Is Difficult

Simply stated, self-compassion is "compassion directed inward" (Germer and Neff 2013). So, there you go. That's it. It should be easy enough, right? Give it a try.

What's that? It's not that easy? Are you confused about what to say and do? First of all, you aren't alone. Self-compassion isn't something we just *do*. There's a lot of interference. In previous chapters, we discussed many reasons why you have fallen into a cyclical habit of reacting with a self-critical voice, even when it increases your emotional pain. There are a lot of factors maintaining your Inner Critic! Recall how you're likely expecting the Inner Critic to keep you from experiencing negative emotions, prevent you from making mistakes, stay part of the group, and maintain your motivation. Here are some more reasons it's so hard to just *do* self-compassion. You may mistake self-compassion for:

- *self-judgment*, the tendency to judge yourself

- *self-pity*, the tendency to become excessively absorbed in your own difficulties

- *self-indulgence*, the act of gratifying yourself too much

How can you distinguish between these obstacles and self-compassion? The most important difference is that self-compassion *moves you forward*, while self-judgment, self-pity, and self-indulgence keep you stuck in the cycle of distress. Have some fun with the next series of exercises, which will quiz your ability to distinguish between these concepts.

Exercise: Who Am I Listening To?

The following statements reflect self-compassion, self-pity, self-indulgence, or self-judgment. Try identifying which is which.

A. "Why am I the one who always has the bad stuff happening to them? It's so unfair."

This is the voice of: _____

B. "Forget it. My kid never listens to me anyway, so why set limits? He's going to do what he's going to do."

This is the voice of: _____

C. "Not getting that promotion feels awful. I'm really disappointed and down. I want to take some time to do what I need to do for myself while I'm sitting with those feelings."

This is the voice of: _____

D. "You're an idiot. Your ideas are stupid, and you always say the wrong thing. That's why no one likes you."

This is the voice of: _____

Key: A. self-pity, B. self-indulgence, C. self-compassion, and D. self-judgment.

Did you get them right? Did discerning between voices feel easy or hard? Write down the things your Inner Critic has said when you thought about doing something kind for yourself.

_____

_____

_____

_____

_____

_____

Exercise: Different Voices

Here are several scenarios of times when we need to call on inner resources for help. Identify what each of the following voices might say in your own mind. We've offered the first one as an example.

1. **Situation:** Holly was on her way to work and ran out of gas.

Self-pitying voice: Why do bad things always happen to me?

Self-indulgent voice: I made a horrible mistake that is too upsetting to go to work. I have to go home and go back to bed.

Self-judgment voice: What an idiot! What kind of adult runs out of gas?!

Self-compassionate voice: Oh gosh. This really sucks. I'm probably not the only person in the world who's done this before.

2. **Situation:** You scheduled an important appointment and completely overlooked it. You missed the appointment.

   Self-pitying voice: _____

   _____

   Self-indulgent voice: _____

   _____

   Self-judgment voice: _____

   _____

   Self-compassionate voice: _____

   _____

3. **Situation:** You were not invited to a dinner party with people in your social circle.

   Self-pitying voice: _____

   _____

   Self-indulgent voice: _____

   _____

   Self-judgment voice: _____

   _____

   Self-compassionate voice: _____

   _____

4. **Situation:** You had an argument in a relationship and now that valuable relationship is over.

Self-pitying voice: _____

_____

Self-indulgent voice: _____

_____

Self-judgment voice: _____

_____

Self-compassionate voice: _____

_____

Look back over the statements you wrote for each voice, in each scenario. Cross out *all* of the statements that might keep you stuck in emotional pain. Are any statements left over?

You may have been taught that extending kindness and acknowledging unpleasant feelings are signs of weakness and vulnerability. Therefore, you may fear others will feel free to prey upon you. Another common thing to learn, mistakenly, is that kindness toward yourself will prevent you from holding yourself accountable for your actions.

Self-compassion is neither of these things. Self-compassion is a stance of nonjudgmental kindness and gentle strength. It can free you up to move forward with dignity. Even when you are in pain, self-compassion will guide you toward experiences that are meaningful and important.

Inviting Self-Compassion

Let's revisit Shawn's story of folding the laundry from the beginning of the chapter. Can you see more clearly how it was an act of self-compassion? Shawn's self-judgment might have been about evaluating and labeling herself "lazy" and "messy." Her self-pity might have centered on the unfairness of doing the laundry because no one else in her house does it. Her self-indulgence might have led her to do one easy chore and then not do anything else for the household the rest of the day, insisting, *They take me for granted, I do too much for them.* Her self-kindness, by contrast, was about choosing what she needed for her well-being. Notice that no punishing labels came with self-kindness. Putting away the laundry was good for Shawn.

What's good for you? The exercises on Listening to Your Self-Compassionate Voice can help you answer that question. Your self-compassionate voice is a sense that some people refer to as *intuition, wise mind, sixth sense,* or *observational self.* We all have this sense inside us; all we have to do is listen to it.

This voice offers to help guide us in the direction of self-compassion. Yet, we don't often listen to it, as we listen to the Inner Critic instead. Part of the problem is that the Inner Critic is louder. The solution is to work with both voices: quiet the Inner Critic and also open your ears to what the compassionate voice has to say. As you practice listening and tuning into yourself, you are in fact learning how to tune out the voice of the Inner Critic. With this in mind, let's come back to exploring the self-compassionate voice.

Exercise: Practicing the Self-Compassionate Voice

In the previous exercise, we provided example scenarios for you to identify your Inner Critic's self-judgmental, self-pitying, and self-indulgent voices. Now recall a time of your own when something you did resulted in a self-judgmental voice. Write what happened.

_____

_____

_____

_____

Write down what you said as you judged yourself. What were the labels you gave yourself? Did you take a black-and-white, right-or-wrong, good-or-bad perspective while self-judging?

_____

_____

_____

Next, write how you would handle this same situation with self-kindness. What would you do differently? How would you speak to yourself differently?

_____

_____

_____

_____

What can you say to yourself in the future when you offer yourself kindness?

_____

_____

_____

Recall a time when something you did resulted in a self-pitying voice. What happened?

_____

_____

What did you say to yourself when you were self-pitying?

_____

_____

_____

What can you say to yourself with self-kindness instead?

_____

_____

_____

Recall a time when you did something that resulted in a self-indulgent voice.

_____

_____

_____

_____

What did you say to yourself when you were self-indulging?

_____

_____

_____

What words of self-kindness can you offer instead?

_____

_____

_____

_____

We hope you are willing to consider that self-compassion is a more effective alternative to self-judgment, self-indulgence, or self-pity. We also hope you are starting to open to the gentler ways you can be with yourself. In the exercise at the beginning of this chapter, titled Compassion for Others, you reflected on a scenario in which you expressed compassion for someone else. Let's look at how the language you use to comfort someone in pain is rarely what you use on yourself.

Exercise: What You'd Never Say to Someone Else

When you are in distress, your Inner Critic likely says some pretty nasty things to you. Yet when your loved ones are suffering, nasty words are probably the last things on your mind. In this exercise, answer the writing prompts, then pause for self-reflection, then repeat. Let's get started!

When you are in distress, what are the five most common things the Inner Critic says to you?

1. _____

2. _____

3. _____

4. _____

5. _____

Would you say those things to a loved one? What do you say instead?

1. _____

2. _____

3. _____

4. _____

5. _____

Now it's time to reflect. As you look at the things you say to yourself that you would never say to another, notice what emotions come up. (Pause)

Notice how you feel in your body. (Pause)

Where in your body do you feel these emotions? (Pause)

What do you imagine the next moments, hours, days, weeks...would be like if you keep saying these things (that you would never say to another) to yourself?

What would happen to your sense of self-worth?

What would happen to trust in yourself? In others?

How could those words impact your relationships?

What appears as you notice? (Pause)

Take a few moments and write down what you noticed as you were reflecting.

_____

_____

_____

_____

Again, look at what you are saying to yourself, how those words make you feel, and ask yourself, *Would I want anyone else to feel the way I am feeling right now*? (Pause)

If the answer is no, which we suspect it is, observe the emotions showing up for you and where you feel them in your body. (Pause)

Now ask yourself: *What would I say to someone else*? Someone who made a mistake, maybe isn't where they want to be in their life, is blaming and shaming themselves for things both out of their control and in their control. (Pause)

We invite you to take a few moments and write down what you would say to them.

_____

_____

_____

_____

Now we invite you to take those same words—with all the emotions and bodily sensations that you may be experiencing—and extend that very same kindness to yourself. You may find this step awkward, challenging, painful, or very emotional. Please know that your experience is common and often part of behavior change.

If you like, place a hand to your heart as you repeat the words you would offer another. (Pause).

Observe what emotions are showing up for you. (Pause)

Now write those words down, along with the feelings, thoughts, and bodily sensations in a message to yourself.

_____

_____

_____

_____

_____

_____

_____

Expressing Compassion for Your Critic

You might be thinking, *What? Compassion for my Inner Critic? You must be crazy!* Hear us out. We have seen—in our own lives and in the lives of our clients—that self-compassion can absolutely tame the Inner Critic.

How? Remember when you have expressed compassion for another person and they softened? They felt seen? They felt supported? The same response happens for your Inner Critic. When you are kind and mindful in the moment, the Inner Critic has very little to say. Let's imagine how this scenario might play out in two common situations in your life. We've provided what Claire experienced as a sample.

Exercise: Responding to the Inner Critic

What is a common situation when you predict the Inner Critic will show up in the next couple of days?

Claire: My monthly check-in and review meeting with my supervisor at work.

How will you use your self-compassionate voice to respond? What will you say?

Claire: It's okay. No one is perfect and we all make some mistakes. Look at all the things she pointed out that I did well. This is a really hard job. I am dedicated and always do my best. I'm proud of myself for that.

After the meeting with her supervisor concluded, Claire came back to this exercise. What was the result? Did her self-compassion stick? Or was it hard to really feel the compassionate voice in the face of the self-critical voice?

Claire: In the moment, I felt like a stupid idiot when she brought up that spreadsheet I couldn't figure out. I was so ashamed I felt like quitting. But then she went over how well I handled that staffing issue for her when she was out sick. After hearing that, I remembered what I promised myself: I can be great at some things and need work on other things. Overall, I'm a good worker and person and my boss likes me. This was the first time that I was able to leave a check-in meeting and not be paralyzed and distracted by feeling ashamed and crappy. Instead, I kind of felt relieved and free. It's easier to get work done.

Now it's your turn. What is a common situation when you predict the Inner Critic will show up in the next couple of days?

_____

_____

How will you use your self-compassionate voice to respond? What will you say?

_____

_____

_____

Come back to this exercise after the situation has concluded. What was the result? Did your self-compassion stick? Or was it hard to really feel the compassionate voice in the face of the self-critical voice?

_____

_____

_____

_____

_____

_____

_____

_____

Let's face it, half the time we're as harsh toward the Inner Critic as it is to us! If you are not in the habit of responding kindly to your Inner Critic, knowing what to say can be downright difficult. Review this list of responses and feel free to draw on them or add your own to the list.

- "I know you're just trying to keep me safe. But it is important that I do this. I've got it!"

- "Thank you for looking out for me. Now I'm going to let The Coach take it from here."

- "It's alright to not be perfect or the best every single time"

- "Hello, Inner Critic, I'm noticing you but I'm _not_ you!"

- "Just because it feels unpleasant doesn't mean something is wrong or bad."

- "Thanks for that information. Duly noted. There's more data that you are overlooking here."

- "I am enough."

- "People value me even when I make mistakes"

- _____
- _____
- _____

Shifting gears in the moment to tune out the Inner Critic and making your self-compassion practice really stick can be challenging. These are skills that must be learned together. We've also been at this very starting point: having read about the benefits of self-compassion and yet not having any idea how to *do* it. Over time, we have taught ourselves, and each other, with some stops and starts. On the bright side, learning that self-compassion is a skill requiring continuous practice has been so transformative for us that it became the motivation to write this book. Here's a process for learning this skill—and as with all new skills, you need to practice, practice, practice.

The Critic's Last Defense

There is likely something inside of you that's still hanging onto the idea that the critical inner voice can be useful. Maybe you're thinking something like, *It keeps me on track and makes sure I don't mess up.* We have heard that from clients many times; in fact, we have also said that to ourselves.

We agree that it's important to hold yourself accountable for doing things that you may regret later. It's also helpful for you to decide on the best course of action to take in a given situation, particularly if an action has potential to cause harm. All this sound logic is what makes this a last defense of the Inner Critic and the trickiest part to navigate.

Remember, the voice of the Inner Critic can fool you into thinking that it is actually helping you. Maybe it seems like it's helping you grow. Or reminding you of the rule we often learn, *What's good for your growth is supposed to hurt.* Or maybe it's telling you something like, *You've got to be cruel to be kind.* We propose something different. Regardless of how an inner voice presents itself, if it causes suffering, holds you to rigid standards, and feels painful, it is not, in fact, helpful. The harsh Inner Critic is not helping you live in ways that are truly based on your values.

What is helpful is a self-compassionate voice of change, or responsibility, that shows you the way to move toward values, vitality, and life satisfaction. This voice holds you to account for changing behaviors that are not working for you, but it does so with kindness and nonjudgmental acceptance. That voice is The Coach. Here is Kay's example of a way to quiet the Inner Critic so The Coach can speak up.

Kay has a long history of suffering as a result of relentless self-criticism. She and her sister were raised by their mother in a small town. They had very little when her parents were married, and after the divorce, when Kay was five and her sister was three years old, they had even less. Their father had always been distant, and he remained absent for most of their lives. As they grew up, the household was abusive and violent, with Kay taking the brunt of her mother's rage while her sister defended their mother and distanced herself from her sister. Kay experienced especially severe injuries at seven years old, when she was sexually abused by a babysitter, and at seventeen, she was raped. Kay pushed the pain so far down inside her that she was sure it would all just go away. But messages of disgust, blame, and loathing became Kay's self-narrative, her inner voice, her most self-incriminating critic.

In adulthood, as a career professional, Kay experienced another traumatic incident on a business trip. While waiting for a table at dinner, a man asked if he could buy her a drink. He seemed nice, well-dressed, handsome, and incredibly respectful. He did all the right things and showed up in all the right ways. But then Kay awoke in a hotel room that wasn't hers with this man on top of her. She could not move, could not scream, and had no recollection of how she got there. When he left, she found herself gathering her things, calling a rideshare, and finding her way back to her hotel. She was violently ill for the next two days, unable to go to work. The logical conclusion was that the man had drugged her drink. Again, she put her emotions aside and "got on" with her life.

Despite her attempts to "push through," Kay began experiencing incredible, seemingly unbearable distress. All her suppressed feelings were surfacing, and she didn't know what to do. She was full of self-blame and self-loathing, punishing herself in hurtful ways. *Why didn't my adult self protect me? Why did I put myself in such a terrible situation? What is wrong with me? I can't ever put myself in this situation again. How did I get here?* This repeated in her head through sobs, as if it was a mantra.

Then Kay began the work of quieting the raging critic in her head, slowing down her narrative in order to transform the self-loathing voice into a more compassionate one. She had kept photos of the man, and when she looked at them, she said all the things she wanted to say to him. Then Kay imagined all the things she would say to someone else who found themselves in her situation. Her inner voice offered gentle understanding, kindness, and compassion. She began to hear the voice of The Coach.

Kay's traumatic events didn't disappear into the ether. Memories surfaced and sometimes became overwhelming. As this happened, the voice of the self-critic became loud again with all the self-loathing and self-blame it brought before. The difference is that now, Kay knows to navigate this resurfaced pain by extending compassion to her vulnerability by coaching herself. Kay has learned to distinguish between the Inner Critic and The Coach. With practice, over time she gets better at putting The Coach into action.

Exercise: Listening to The Coach

Recall a time when your Inner Critic had you suffer before a period of growth happened. For example, say you went through a breakup. Maybe you experienced self-loathing at first, then you worked on your relational skills and, a few months later, began a much stronger relationship with someone else.

Briefly describe a situation that caused you pain.

_____

_____

_____

_____

As best as you can, write down the messages, rules, and criticisms your Inner Critic served up.

_____

_____

_____

_____

_____

_____

_____

Now write down what it would've sounded like if you'd spoken to yourself with the voice of The Coach instead. Perhaps your inner coach did speak up in that situation, in the course of your growth. As you write, consider The Coach's messages of kindness, common humanity, and mindful awareness. Use the things you would say to another human being in your situation as examples.

_____

_____

_____

_____

_____

_____

_____

_____

When you access your inner coach, you are accessing self-compassion. While the Inner Critic may shout, react, remind you of rules, criticize, punish, and compare you to others, The Coach will guide you to observe what's happening, identify what you're feeling and thinking, envision what you might like to do or see happen in a situation, practice the skills you need to get you to that place, and stick to things in inspired ways. These are the same elements that make up a self-compassion practice!

We'll dive into each of these elements in detail for the remainder of the book. In chapter 5, we're going to help you increase your skills of observation and mindful awareness. We'll then build on those skills in chapter 6 to help you envision and identify what moves you forward, brings meaning to your days, and adds vitality to your life. In chapter 7, we'll show what it takes to stay committed when things get confusing and rough. And chapter 8 wraps up with ways to create a committed and consistent plan to practice ongoing self-compassion.

In contrast to the rigid, harsh, punishing tone of the Inner Critic, a self-compassionate voice brings kindness and mindful awareness of just how universal the experience of emotional pain is for all human beings. While you may have the capacity to extend compassion to others, it is sometimes difficult and uncomfortable to offer it to yourself. Quieting the critical and demanding voice that thinks it's helping—but that ends up causing more suffering—involves extending compassion, kindness, common humanity, and mindfulness to yourself. By doing so, you discover a voice that doesn't leave you feeling battered and bruised and spinning in distressing circles. Instead, your Inner Coach leads you in the meaningful directions that you want to travel. In the coming chapters, you'll practice extending that kind and gentle stance toward yourself by learning how to use specific skills. The next chapter will help you expand your mindful awareness and observation.

CHAPTER 5

Observe the Critic's Effects

As you pivot from self-criticism to the self-compassion that results from listening to your Inner Coach, it helps immensely to be able to observe *when* you need to make that pivot. In order to observe your behavior, you must learn how to notice yourself An *observer* is someone who pays attention to something, who watches with awareness. While observing, there is an expectation of a nonjudgmental stance and mindful awareness of your responses. Observing in this non-judgmental way allows you to *respond* to situations rather than *react* to them like the Inner Critic does.

To help you practice being an observer of the situations you find yourself in, as well as the reactions of your critical inner voice, you can use the acronym CARE. This stands for the basic steps of observing in the moment: *connect, allow, respond,* and *embrace.*

Through the course of this chapter, your consistent and compassionate practice of CARE will help you observe behaviors that happen on the inside—your thoughts, feelings, and bodily sensations—and the actionable behaviors that occur outside of you. As you practice these skills, you'll get better and better at observing the ways the Inner Critic steers you to behave, so you can choose compassionate and values-based behaviors instead.

Reacting Versus Responding

All too often, we *react* to what is happening in the moment rather than *respond* to it. There's a profound difference between them. Responding is acting intentionally in the moment based upon what we are noticing. Reacting is acting on our *interpretation of* what is happening in the moment. Let's look at an example of a reactive conversation between Holly and her husband.

Holly tells her husband, "Let's make sure the recycling gets down to the curb. Last time it didn't get put out in time and piled up."

Her husband's jaw drops. "Really? I always take the recycling down. You're saying I never do? Great, I'm a terrible husband. Whatever."

Holly defends herself by saying, "What are you talking about? You never hear me and always think the worst of me!"

Miscommunication and distress are now front and center, and an argument is on. What if it had gone another way? Let's look at how it might unfold if Holly and her husband respond to each other instead.

Holly's husband might nod, "Okay, we can get it to the curb. If you don't put it down there, I will make sure I do."

That sounds pretty straightforward, yes? Well, let's now suppose that he assumed Holly was implying that he didn't take out the recycling.

He scratches his head and asks, "Are you saying that I don't ever put it down? It kinda feels like that's what you're saying."

Holly can then clarify. "No, that's not what I mean at all. We forgot last time, so I want to get it down this time."

That is pretty effective communication. It's more likely to prevent an argument or misunderstanding. In these examples, *reacting* is based on inaccurate information and can lead to a distress cycle. *Responding*, however, allows you to notice not only what behavior is currently being presented, but also your own interpretations and opportunities to see if you are accurate. In the last exchange, Holly and her husband were skillfully able to *respond*, and the recycling got to the curb.

While this example is rather benign, no matter how simple a behavior is, we are humans with histories and stories we tell ourselves about who we are. When that leads to an assumption, suffering becomes front and center, which is the Inner Critic talking.

When we act on what we think or feel about a situation or interaction before we have enough information, it is incredibly confusing. It doesn't give us an opportunity to make an accurate decision. It directs us to follow ineffective pathways. It interferes with how we identify what is important and leads us away from the ways we want to show up in life. In order to more accurately assess what is actually happening, you can practice being the observer. This will allow you to respond to what is happening in the moment rather than reacting to your interpretations of it.

The exercises you've done so far have already prepared you to be the observer of your behavior. You have been paying attention, on purpose, with intention and nonjudgmental awareness. You're right on track.

Observing a Larger Context

Let's return to Shawn's situation with her group of friends, from chapter 2, in which she was trying to participate in the conversation and wound up blurting out her opinion. Some more data about that scenario emerges when we view it in *context*. That is, perceiving all the situational factors happening at the time.

In reality, Shawn's friends like her very much. They are loving and supportive, and weren't judging how she was interacting at the gathering. If you were an observer—a fly on the wall, so to speak—you might notice that they seemed to be paying less attention to Shawn because she was disengaging from them. They perceived her behavior as disinterested, without anything to say. If you asked around, you might find out that one of the women even thought *she* had done something wrong to make Shawn lose interest in the conversation (the result of her own Inner Critic!).

In this case, Shawn's Inner Critic was incorrectly assuming emotional danger arising from a social "mistake." Her Inner Critic was on automatic pilot based on past learning with other women friends who *had* invalidated and hurt her. The story her Inner Critic shouted at her was that making "social mistakes" would be painful. As a result, Shawn missed out on the rest of a meaningful evening because she listened to her critical voice obediently, without question.

Do you think Shawn was *responding* to the actual situation or *reacting* to her immediate perception of it? Consider how much pain Shawn might have avoided if she looked at the situation with an observer's eye. By intentionally observing, it is possible to take in more context within situations, gain more data, and use that to counterbalance the voice of the Inner Critic.

Certainly, your threat detection system can respond accurately. And at times, you may be unable to discern whether it is or is not telling tales. This is one of the reasons why quieting and disarming the critical voice can be so very tough. It's also why it's important to respond by observing situational data nonjudgmentally and then consciously choosing how you respond to the data you observe. Essentially, you can't always believe the Inner Critic and you certainly do not always have to listen to it obediently.

So, what did Shawn eventually do to quiet her Inner Critic? She became the observer in order to move from self-critical to self-compassionate.

- Here are the judgments that she observed arising: *You've been rude! You've been loud! Why'd you blurt that out? It was a dumb thing to say! They must think you're an attention-seeker!*

- She observed how she felt compelled to act as a result: clam up, stay quiet, and make herself small.

- Last, she understood the problem at hand: her Inner Critic was speaking up because it assumed a social mistake had happened, but it was incorrectly perceiving the context.

With these insights, Shawn can indeed clam up, stay quiet, and make herself small. She can go on beating herself up, wondering why that voice keeps interfering with her relationships and how she feels about herself. But that doesn't sound pleasant or productive. We are betting that you would prefer she take another course of action.

Shawn gained insight into the perceived danger and assumptions her Inner Critic was automatically making. They were incorrect and leading her away from her values. This realization can help her consciously turn toward The Coach for compassion.

You too can take this course of action in similar self-critical situations. That's where CARE comes in. Think of it as a four-step process for switching into observer mode, even in complex or charged situations that really rev up your self-critic. These steps will help you put self-compassion into practice.

Connect with yourself

Allow whatever thoughts, feelings, and bodily sensations you are experiencing to be present

Respond to yourself with kindness

Embrace what is happening in the moment (without judgment)

As you start this practice, we invite you to write the steps out in this workbook. The hope is that the more you practice, the more this skill and its steps will be integrated into how you move through the world. Eventually, you'll no longer need to write anything. Someday, when the Inner Critic bellows like a beast, the practice of CARE will help you tame it—in that very moment.

Exercise: The Four Steps to a Self-Compassionate Voice

Let's walk through the exercise in a general sense so you can build awareness to observe when, where, and how the Inner Critic shows up. You can download and print the steps for this exercise at http://www.newharbinger.com/54292.

Step 1: Connect

Find a place to be still, put your hand over your heart, and focus your attention on your breath going in and going out. *Connect* with your experience in this moment. It doesn't matter where you are; you can be among other people, alone, standing or seated, with eyes closed or open. You are *slowing down,* centering or grounding yourself, and finding a mindful way to be with yourself intentionally without judgment. You are creating space to be with whatever is happening.

Record what you connected with and observed. What thoughts or images arose?

_____

_____

_____

_____

What feelings did you connect with?

_____

_____

_____

What did you connect with in your body?

_____

_____

_____

Now go back to your sense of connection with yourself. As you do, remember this is a go-to skill that you can use whenever you need to tame the critical inner voice. Let's explore the next step.

Step 2: Allow

By slowing down and bringing mindful attention to what is happening right here, right now, *allow* whatever thoughts, feelings, and bodily sensations you are experiencing to surface. There is no need to push them away. Instead, give them permission and approval. You can give yourself permission to let whatever experiences you are having to come. Then take a moment to write about it.

What did you notice? Describe what you *allowed* to surface.

_____

_____

_____

Was there anything you struggled to allow? Anything that your mind prevented you from accessing? Write about how that struggle or block felt.

_____

_____

_____

Return to allowing your experience to arise in this moment. Notice what's happening inside you; let it be as it is. When you're ready, move on to the next step.

Step 3: Respond

It is often automatic to react to our experiences with harsh words and punishing attitudes. Here, you're going to practice doing the opposite. You are going to respond to yourself with kindness and tenderness. You'll start this practice by filling out a chart, which will slow down your habitual thoughts and give you a chance to use your Connect and Allow skills.

Write any thoughts that have a punishing tone in the first column of the chart. In the other column, see if you can write kinder, more tender ways of speaking to yourself. If you are able to immediately write a kind, loving response in the second column—great!

Harsh Thought	Tender Thought

Can you imagine what it would be like, even for a moment, to automatically respond to your experience with tender kindness? That is a lofty goal, we know, because thoughts, feelings and memories continue to stay with us. We don't get to hit a delete button. It may seem impossible to leave behind the habitual reactions you have used for so long. Consider, then, that you can choose to *add* new ways to talk to yourself. You are adding skills and broadening them to quiet the critical voice and allow the kind, tender voice to speak to you in ways that capture your attention. That is our wish for you—our wish for all of us.

Step 4: Embrace

To *embrace* means to hold closely, accept and support willingly, and welcome with open arms. This makes embracing our experience the simplest step, and the most difficult. It's simple because the things that human beings experience just show up; there is not a lot we have to do there. But we are judgmental creatures, which makes meeting what shows up with openness difficult. Recall that resisting your internal experience, or perceiving it as dangerous or threatening, opens the door to the Inner Critic and its reactions. Letting your experience, whatever it happens to be, be there so you can *accept* it opens the space for The Coach, for compassion, and for responding.

Try embracing your experience of this very moment. Notice what happens within you, and then write about what happened.

_____

_____

_____

_____

_____

_____

_____

_____

The first step in CARE is to connect. You just practiced connecting with yourself. However, we are social creatures who thrive with connection to others. The Harvard Happiness Study found that one of the biggest predictors of a long and happy life is deep bonds with loved ones (Newall et al. 2009). Other researchers and experts also tell us that the power of connection is one of the keys to happiness and increased quality of living.

Yet, connecting can feel so hard to do. The Inner Critic can interfere with your desire to be authentic with others, leaving you feeling lonely, vulnerable, and unfulfilled. Because close relationships are central to emotional well-being, we invite you to see where you may have an opportunity to connect with others. We aren't saying that every connection needs to be deep or intense. You don't need to run out scoping for a new BFF. Nor are we suggesting that you need to connect with anyone and everyone.

We are asking you to simply notice how you may be holding back in your relationships. How might your Inner Critic be preventing you from reaching out to others? Where could it be blocking opportunities for the vulnerability that leads to connection?

Exercise: Start Connecting with Others

Here is a list of connection resources. Put a checkmark next to the ones you are familiar with and can access. If you have a place in mind where you can connect with people that isn't on this list, add your own.

- ☐ place of worship
- ☐ book club
- ☐ community sports team (pickleball, tennis, softball)
- ☐ gym
- ☐ classes and events at a local community college or library
- ☐ yoga class
- ☐ special interest hobby group (cooking clubs, hiking groups)
- ☐ meditation group
- ☐ workplace
- ☐ parents of your child's classmates
- ☐ neighbors
- ☐ civic organizations and activities
- ☐ volunteer activities
- ☐ acting and improv groups
- ☐ _____
- ☐ _____
- ☐ _____

Once you have identified areas of interest, consider making the connections. You may notice fear, uncertainty, and the voice of your critic arising. Using the steps of CARE, let's walk through the courageous steps of creating connections, this time with other people.

Exercise: Making the Connection

Once again, we'll guide you through a four-step process.

Step 1: Connect

Find a place to be still, put your hand over your heart, and focus your attention on your breath going in and going out. It doesn't matter where you are—you can be among other people, alone, standing or seated, with eyes closed or open. You are *slowing down,* centering or grounding yourself, and finding a mindful way to be with yourself and others intentionally without judgment. You are creating space for whatever is happening in the moment.

When you are grounded in the present moment, shift your attention to the meaningful sense of connection with others. What might you gain by connecting with people?

_____

_____

What might it cost you? Record your fears, offering kind attention to your experience as you write them down. What is your Inner Critic saying?

_____

_____

_____

_____

What might it cost you if you do not connect? Are there any benefits for choosing to not connect?

_____

_____

_____

_____

Listen carefully to the part of you that wants to connect. Is the voice of The Coach moving you toward reaching out to others? Write down what your kind, compassionate coach is saying.

_____

_____

_____

_____

Step 2: Allow

As you slow down and put mindful attention on what is happening right here, right now, *allow* whatever thoughts, feelings and bodily sensations you are experiencing to surface. There is no need to push them away. Give yourself permission and approval to let whatever experiences you are having come.

This is a moment of choice. Your knowledge of the difference between expected function versus actual function becomes important, so take a minute to circle back. The Inner Critic and The Coach both want to keep you safe. The paradox is that the critical voice keeps you away from a life of purpose and meaning. Whereas The Coach leads you in the direction of what will ultimately heal. The Coach knows you might get hurt *and* that you are more likely to find connection.

Observe the thoughts, feelings, and bodily sensations that come up as you consider taking action toward connecting with others. See if you can make space for all that. Write down what shows up.

_____

_____

_____

_____

_____

Is there anything you struggled to allow? Anything that your mind prevented you from accessing? Write some words to describe what that struggle or block felt like.

_____

_____

_____

_____

Step 3: Respond

Next, consider your experience. Write down what you heard the Inner Critic say about connecting with other people. Then write down the messages coming from The Coach.

Voice of the Inner Critic	Voice of The Coach

Step 4: Embrace

Now, given all that the Inner Critic probably said, you might have compelling reasons to play it safe and not connect with others. And you also have compelling reasons to connect with them. We invite you to acknowledge the Inner Critic and any of the painful feelings that come with its critical voice. Then, move in the direction of vitality and meaning anyway. In other words, as convincing as the Inner Critic is, you can listen to The Coach instead. Authentic connections are guided by this kind, supportive voice.

Describe what it would be like if you acknowledged the Inner Critic but listened to The Coach—and chose connection anyway. What might you do, say, and feel?

_____

_____

_____

_____

_____

_____

_____

_____

_____

The scenario you imagined is possible for you! We are cheering you on to keep listening to your Coach.

We have spent time observing, imagining, and feeling. Now, you get to take some action. You don't have to start big. Big often stops us. Instead, let's start small.

Exercise: Start with a Small Step

What is the next small step The Coach is suggesting you take? We'll give you some ideas to get you started and, as always, feel free to add your own.

- Pick up the phone

- Go to the website and fill out the registration

- Send an email

- Walk over to the community center

- _____

- _____

- _____

- _____

- _____

Whatever that very first step is, we encourage you to take it.

You can also use CARE to respond to your experiences of emotional pain, in the present moment, with loving-kindness and self-compassion. The following guided exercise is a gentle introduction to practicing mindful, nonjudgmental awareness of your distress.

Exercise: Tending Your Pain

Sometimes it's necessary to go *toward* painful experiences in order to heal. This exercise is one of those times. You can download a guided audio recording of this exercise at http://www.newharbin ger.com/54292. Find a quiet spot where you will not be interrupted for about fifteen minutes. Allow your eyes to gently close or find a spot in front of you to focus on with a soft gaze.

Begin by taking several, slow, deep breaths. Breathe in fully and exhale slowly. Begin to shift your attention from outside to inside yourself, letting go of noises around you. If you are distracted by sounds in the room, simply notice this and bring your focus back to your breathing. Feel the sensations of breathing: Your stomach expanding on an inhale and relaxing as you exhale. Notice the rise and fall of your shoulders with each inhale and exhale. Pay attention to what those sensations feel like. Take three more breaths like this, noticing sensations in your body.

Turn your attention to memories, images, and thoughts. Recall a time recently when you experienced shame. Maybe it happened during an interaction with someone important to you or a conversation that did not go as you would have liked.

When you have that experience in mind, see if you can recreate the scene in your mind's eye. Try to visualize and re-experience what was happening, what you looked like, what you were thinking, what you were feeling. See if you can connect with the self-critical thoughts that came up in that moment. What was your Inner Critic saying to you or shouting at you? Can you notice the hurtful words?

As you are reconnecting with those self-critical thoughts, are you able to notice what your body is doing? Where in your body are you experiencing that deep pain of shame? Perhaps in your chest? Or your stomach? Try to notice and allow whatever sensations are coming up. How would you describe them with words? Do you feel "pressure"? An "aching" feeling? A "tenseness"? When you are able to locate where in your body you most feel shame, place one hand gently on that area. Continue to connect with those sensations.

As you stay connected with the sensations of shame, see if you can imagine how much space that center of pain takes up. Does it cover a large area? Bigger than a fist? A tiny spot the size of an eraser? Can you see its size in your mind's eye? As you continue observing your pain, imagine that it has a shape. Is it round? A cube? Maybe it has an irregular shape. What do you see in your mind's eye?

Staying focused on the area of your body that holds shame, imagine touching it. What sort of texture would it have? Rough or scratchy? Soft or smooth? Notice its temperature. Burning hot? Body temperature? Icy cold? Stay focused on what it feels like to touch your shame, as it is, in your body.

What would it feel like to hold it in your hand? Light? Hard and heavy, like a rock? Stay focused on these sensations for a few more moments. Imagine that the hand touching that place in your body is actually holding your place of pain—holding your own pain. Notice what comes up for you as your hand rests there. Do you want to fling it across the room? Stuff it way down inside? Notice any tenderness toward it, coming from your hand. Feel any tenderness toward yourself, as your hand rests on your pain. Stay with this moment. See if you can connect with your pain—and yourself—with tenderness.

Still holding your hand on this point of pain, draw your attention to other feelings. What does it feel like to be holding your pain in your hand? Does it cause you more pain? Stay with this feeling a bit longer. Does the pain change at all? When you give yourself permission to make room for the pain, it will fade. Even if it comes back, it will fade long enough for you to take a small step forward to heal. As challenging as it is to make room for the pain, the more you fight it, the bigger it gets.

Take three slow, deep breaths. Take whatever time you need before slowly opening your eyes. Then consider your responses to the following questions.

Write to your pain. What is it telling you? What do you want your pain to know about how it is affecting you? This is an opportunity to separate yourself from your pain. If there was no pain, write about that experience.

_____

_____

_____

_____

_____

_____

_____

This is another way to bring compassion to your Inner Critic, to quiet it in ways that care for your pain in a compassionate way, without any harshness or demeaning and demoralizing messages. It's a way of humanizing your pain. Recall that one of the attributes of self-compassion is common humanity. By humanizing your pain, you are, in fact, bringing compassion to it.

The next time you find yourself in a situation where your Inner Critic pipes up, see if you can apply the CARE steps in the moment. Explore connecting with yourself and others in the moment, allowing whatever arises to be there with acceptance, responding to yourself and the situation with kindness and a sense of your values, and embracing what's happening in the moment.

Afterward, come back to this workbook and write about the experience. How did it unfold for you, in new ways?

_____

_____

_____

_____

_____

_____

_____

When you are exploring the difference between reacting and responding, it's helpful to remember that the stories you tell yourself—your history—can play a role. In chapter 1, you learned about the narratives you formed as your younger self to keep yourself safe and out of harm's way. You explored how those narratives may no longer be useful now. How can you know they are no longer useful? Because they are causing you pain and suffering as an adult. Your Inner Critic is relying on old information and old contexts. What _will_ work now? You can revise and update your story to reflect what you want your life to be about now!

Exercise: Revising Your Story

In the space offered here, or in a separate journal, we invite you to reflect on your history. You can return to the history you relayed in chapter 1 as part of the exercise Writing Down Your History, if that's helpful. As you write a new story, allow yourself to notice if reliving parts of your history are prolonging your pain and suffering. If pain comes, see if you can care for yourself using the CARE skills. Given your history, where you stand right now, with all the work you've done to quiet your Inner Critic and the self-compassion skills you've been tapping into, what do you want your story to be from here?

What is the story you want to guide your life from here? Write it now.

_____

_____

_____

_____

_____

_____

_____

_____

_____

_____

_____

_____

_____

_____

_____

_____

_____

Now reflect on what that was like. How do you feel writing about what you *want* your life to be like?

_____

_____

_____

Was it easy to envision? What do you see yourself doing differently as a result?

_____

_____

_____

If you had difficulty picturing what a forward-moving life might look like, write about what inner obstacles are still in your way.

_____

_____

_____

Being able to identify who and how you want to be in your life helps you establish purpose for your actions. When the Inner Critic's voice pipes up to tell you how to *react* (and it will!), if you have clarity of purpose, you can leverage that purpose to *respond* to situations in ways that take you in forward-moving directions that are meaningful and vital, instead of staying safe and staying stuck in the past.

First, we want to share a powerful way to track your behavior change. Tracking is a great practice that helps you notice patterns, forces you to be more in the present, and gives you vital information about progressing or slipping. Because it is so easy to fall back into old, familiar patterns of behavior, it's important to practice observing the effects that transformation has on us. Use the following worksheet to track your reactions and responses, if you find it helpful. You can download this worksheet at http://www.newharbinger.com/54292 to create as many copies as you need.

Exercise: Transforming the Inner Critic

Situation: _____

_____

_____

_____

What my Inner Critic said: _____

_____

_____

_____

How I felt: _____

_____

_____

_____

Did I react or respond? How so? _____

_____

_____

_____

What parts of the CARE steps did I do? _____

_____

_____

_____

How the CARE steps worked for me: _____

_____

_____

_____

Did I tap into The Coach in the process? What did that kind, compassionate voice say?

_____

_____

_____

_____

_____

This chapter focused on how to be the observer of your own behaviors, watching with awareness and nonjudgment. With the CARE steps, you can be present with yourself and other people to respond in the moment, rather than react based on your interpretation of what's happening. Reacting all too often leads to disconnection and misunderstanding, keeping you stuck in patterns of suffering and inadequacy. Responding frees you to take action in the pursuit of a life of purpose. The next chapter will help you continue to identify what matters to you, so that, as you become practiced at responding to your Inner Critic with CARE, you will know what choices to respond with and why.

CHAPTER 6

Identify What Matters More Than What Your Inner Critic Says

We have explored how the Inner Critic hurts us. Makes us feel small. Inadequate. Ashamed. How it keeps us from people and opportunities to try things, take risks, love boldly, act with confidence in ourselves, and be the kind of people we want to be. When we listen to that harsh voice, we disconnect from so much that is alive and rich because that's how our Inner Critic would have it.

Yet, if shame and isolation and fear and feelings of inadequacy weren't standing in the way, what would you be doing instead? This chapter invites you to explore what is important to you. Your *needs* may come to mind, such as food, clothing, and shelter—all important to keep you alive. But beyond the basics, what feels fulfilling and meaningful? By answering these questions, then acting based on what is important to you, you gain direct access to The Coach. This supportive voice likes nothing more than to guide you in directions that are meaningful to you. This is also one of the most powerful ways to quiet the Inner Critic.

The Important Things in Life

We invite you to give yourself space to consider some questions: What makes your heart sing? What brings fulfillment, meaning, and a sense of purpose to your days? What do you want life to be about? How do you wish to *be* in the world? As you explore what matters most to you, let your heart lead. Your Inner Critic may start piping up, saying something like, *Why are you doing this? You're no good at these things, anyway!* Remember to CARE for yourself. You might reply, *I know you're just trying to keep me safe and free from hurt. And now, it's The Coach's turn to talk!*

The following exercise can be difficult. The critical inner voice has a way of devaluing what's important to you or steering you away from what you most want to do. We want you to know that not only do your values matter, they are a critical part of a life well lived.

Exercise: What Makes Your Soul Dance and Your Heart Sing?

Write down as many things as you can think of that make your soul dance. These could be:

- activities (playing with pets, hiking)

- places (the beach, music concert)

- moments in your life that have felt profoundly special or meaningful (volunteering in your community, stargazing)

- qualities of living—how you want to move through the world (being kind, exercising curiosity)

- activities and experiences that used to bring meaning and instill joy, but you stopped doing for one reason or another

- whatever you think you would find moving, even if you haven't experienced it before

Remember, what makes your soul dance is unique to you. It's not about what is expected of you, it's about what *you* most value.

1. _____

2. _____

3. _____

4. _____

5. _____

6. _____

7. _____

8. _____

9. _____

10. _____

What was it like to think of the things that bring you joy? Did you have difficulty identifying many? Or were you able to tap into a range of experiences? Write down what you noticed.

_____

_____

_____

What, if anything, surprised you as you listed sources of meaning and purpose?

_____

_____

_____

Review your list. Next to each item, write a few words explaining what about it brings you joy. How does it make you feel? What does it reflect about you? Note how it contributes to your life.

If that exercise was challenging and you couldn't come up with as many experiences as you'd like, or you're not sure if those things *really* make your heart sing, here's another activity to try. The following exercise targets your potential regrets as cues for what you value. You see, studies of the elderly have shown that their biggest regrets are failing to do things they wished they had done, but hadn't (Newall et al. 2009). Reasons they didn't pursue desired experiences included choosing to play it safe, being stopped by uncertainty, or facing challenges they saw as barriers. The next exercise can help you identify what matters to you by envisioning regrets.

Exercise: What Do You Want It to Be About?

For this exercise, find a quiet spot where you will not be interrupted or distracted for about ten minutes. You can listen to an audio recording of this guided exercise at http://www.newharbinger .com/54292. Listening to the audio version is highly recommended. Afterward, respond to the writing prompt.

Sit in a comfortable position and close your eyes. Take a few breaths, mindful of what it feels like to breathe in and out. Then, in your mind's eye, imagine yourself seated in a large space, surrounded by all of the people in your life who you have appreciated and loved, and whose lives have interconnected with yours. These people can be alive today or they may have already passed. Let it come into awareness that you are the guest of honor at your own ninety-ninth birthday party and these people have gathered to celebrate and honor you—and the life you have lived. Each one in turn shares experiences that speak to what, if any, impact you have had on them, what you mean to them, and what kind of life you have led.

What do they say about you? When you are ready, open your eyes and write your response.

_____

_____

_____

_____

_____

This exercise illustrates what truly matters to you. Seeing yourself through the eyes of others—how they see you allocate your attention and energy—allows you to recognize disconnections that may exist between how you actually engage with the world and how it might look for you to be living the vital, purpose-driven life you want. Let's take a look at how the exercise helped Claire clarify what really brings her life meaning.

Claire's experience with this exercise felt powerful to her. She described an emotional moment when her grandchildren shared who she was to them.

"Grandma has always been really quiet," her granddaughter said.

Her grandson described her this way: "She's a quiet and jumpy old lady."

Claire began to cry during the exercise and shouted, "No! That's not right! They should know that I love them so much and that I'm really kind. And a good listener. And creative! And talented!"

After the exercise, Claire was very excited and the words tumbled out of her onto the page. She wrote about the joy she used to feel creating watercolors in middle school. When other students would admire her artwork, calling it beautiful and Claire talented, she felt proud and accomplished. Claire began wondering why she had stopped painting. She decided to buy paints and paper later that week.

As Claire painted with watercolors again, her growing sense of fulfillment was far greater than merely spending time engaged in a pleasant activity. The energy and enthusiasm of her renewed creativity had her "looking for the beauty in the world because there is so much out there to see." She painted a watercolor card depicting a path in the woods with butterflies. Inside, she wrote, "I have found the way to become the beautiful person I have always wanted me to be."

Your response to this exercise may not be as strong or obvious as Claire's was. That's okay. Sometimes it's easier to figure out what we *don't* want our lives to look like. When Shawn first tried this exercise, she envisioned her son saying, "I'll remember my mom best for having a clean kitchen floor." It remains a family joke that whenever she does something meaningful with her son, someone says, "Guess the kitchen isn't getting mopped today!"

Did your envisioning include things you don't want to be remembered for? Qualities that others see on the outside, but that don't reflect your inner world—your true self? What do you want to be remembered for that wasn't brought up? Write them down.

_____

_____

_____

_____

_____

This reflection can help increase your awareness of qualities of yourself that you might be overlooking or ignoring, perhaps unknowingly. This is helpful! Because you now have the chance to put what truly matters to *you* into action *now*. You don't have to think, *I wish I could have [done/been/seen] that and I didn't.*

Identifying Your Values

In the previous two exercises, you listed things that bring meaning to your life and that you want to be remembered for. Let's consider what those things have in common. Likely, it's your *values*. Values are the qualities or principles that guide how you want to move through life. They represent the sort of person you want to be and what you want your life to be about. So what are your values? Try doing the next couple of exercises to find out.

Exercise: Your Life Domains

One way to identify what matters to you is to consider the life domains that are most important to you or bring meaning and vitality to your days. These may change over time, based on evolving circumstances. For this reason, it's helpful to come back to this exercise several times. Take a look at the following chart and follow these steps.

Step 1: In the middle column, rate each of the following values domains according to how *important* these aspects of your life are: 1 is least important and 10 is most important. You are not rank ordering them, so you can use numbers more than once. Be sure to rate their importance to *you*, not how you think you are supposed to rank them based on family or social expectations.

Step 2: In the third column, rate each of the domains based on how you *prioritize* them in your daily life: 1 has the lowest priority and 10 has the highest priority. For this area, you are rating how much time or energy you're giving to it in a day, compared to other tasks, regardless of its importance to you. For example, Shawn consistently rates recreation at a 9 on the *importance* scale, but alas engaged in very few leisure activities while writing this book, so her rating is a 2 on the *priority* scale. Again, you are not rank ordering them, so you can use numbers more than once.

Values Domain	Importance	Priority
Family		
Marriage, partner(s), intimate relationships		
Parenting		
Friendships and social life		
Career and employment		
Education and personal growth		
Recreation, fun, leisure		
Spirituality		
Citizenship, environment, community		
Health: physical and mental well-being		

Now compare how you rated the importance and prioritization of your values. Where do you see mismatches? For example, if you value *citizenship* as an 8 but prioritize it as a 3, that indicates a disparity. Reflect on your mismatches. Why do you think they are there? Consider whether your Inner Critic is playing a role in this as you respond.

_____

_____

_____

_____

_____

Now that you have started thinking about what aspects of life hold meaning and purpose for you, we invite you to consider specific qualities of who and how you want to be that bring vitality to your life.

Exercise: The Language of Values

Look through the following list of qualities. Place a checkmark next to those you most want to embody. Try to identify at least six. Feel free to add words of your own if you can't find one on the list that fits.

☐ accomplishment	☐ creativity	☐ honesty
☐ adventure	☐ curiosity	☐ independence
☐ authenticity	☐ equality	☐ integrity
☐ beauty	☐ excellence	☐ kindness
☐ being loved	☐ excitement	☐ love
☐ caring	☐ faith	☐ loyalty
☐ challenge	☐ fame	☐ material well-being
☐ compassion	☐ flexibility	☐ nurturing
☐ conformity	☐ forgiveness	☐ openness
☐ connection	☐ fun	☐ power
☐ contemplation	☐ genuineness	☐ service
☐ contribution	☐ gratitude	☐ teaching or mentoring
☐ courage		☐ trust

Write down any of the qualities on the list that immediately jumped out as being important to you.

Are there themes that your values have in common? For example, say in the previous exercise you listed parenting, marriage, and family as your top values domains. Then here, you identified kindness, loyalty, and being loved as your top values. You might decide they have common themes of connection, love, intimacy, vulnerability, and safety. What themes do you notice?

Sometimes we have been taught what qualities "should be" important by someone else. They may or may not actually bring you a sense of meaning and purpose. Consider whether your Inner Critic is telling you what should or should not be important. Write down your thoughts about this.

Look at the qualities you chose. Are you currently bringing these qualities to the life domains you previously identified as important? Reflect on this here.

If you're aware that you are not bringing these qualities to your important life domains, write down why you think that might be the case. Is your Inner Critic steering you away? Consider that you may be avoiding painful emotions, rules, or stories that tell you that you can't act with these qualities. Or perhaps you fear all the ways you will fail if you do.

_____

_____

_____

_____

If you find you are not living your values as fully as you would like, know that you are not alone. Many people struggle with this. Still, it can be disheartening to see that the things you value are being pushed to the back burner, perhaps without your awareness. By learning how to identify disparities, you can now work toward prioritizing the things that matter to you! The rest of this chapter walks you through how to do just that.

From Knowing Your Values to Doing Your Values

How can you know you are "doing" what you value? So far, you have identified what values are important to you. Now, we'll help you generate the action steps required to move in the direction of what you value. And as you do, we'll offer ways to determine whether or not you are staying on the right track.

This is where goals can come in. If values are the *qualities* of action that feel important to how you want to live your life, goals are the step-by-step *actions* you take. Along the way, *benchmarks* help you confirm that you are living life the way you want to.

Setting Goals

In order to *do* your values, it helps to come up with a list of steps to take that reflect those values. These are your goals. Identifying the steps needed to work toward your values can be daunting. There are numerous techniques for how to concretely set goals, such as SMART goals and the PACT method, to name just a couple. Since this section of the workbook is specifically addressing how to identify action steps for moving in the direction of your values, we will only highlight a very basic framework to use.

Creating a list of action steps that will help you move in the direction of what is meaningful involves two basic steps:

1. identifying target actions

2. putting them in a manageable sequence

Some tasks lend themselves to a specific order of steps. Baking a cake, for example, usually involves the following actions and sequence: 1) measuring ingredients such as flour, baking powder, and liquid; 2) mixing them together; 3) baking the mixture in an oven. If you perform these steps in a different sequence, or choose different actions, you won't end up with a cake. Imagine stirring the flour, putting the milk in the freezer, and sprinkling the baking powder in the oven. Not a cake!

When contemplating how to take action toward your values, you fortunately have much greater freedom than a dessert chef! Because you choose the qualities of action and the substance of your valued experiences, you get to decide how you want to get there. For example, if we asked you, "Who do you love?" you would probably come up with a list of at least a few people. If we then asked you, "Do they know you love them?" you'd likely say yes. If we ask you *how* those people know you love them, you would hopefully respond with a list of things you say and actions you take that let them know.

In other words, the message "I love you" is a set of actions. By engaging in those verbal or nonverbal behaviors that signal your loving for them, they know they are loved. People demonstrate and perceive lovingness in unique ways. Some might offer acts of kindness, such as routinely having coffee ready for a partner in the morning. Others may help a friend solve a social problem without judgment or rejection. Parents might, in a calm steady voice, say "I love you" to a tantruming toddler, while a spouse might grab their partner's hand after an argument and whisper, "We'll be alright."

On the other hand, when we ask how people know you love them, you could say, "Well they just know, I don't tell them or hug or anything because we don't do that in our family." Then we would wonder if they know. In this example, loving is a value, and when you don't take action toward what matters to you, it likely won't be realized.

There aren't many ways around the *doing* part. You must *do* the thing that matters to *create* the thing that matters. We have given you a few examples of what "doing" loving can look like. Now it's your turn to generate what "doing" your values might look like in action.

Exercise: Envisioning Valued Actions

Review the qualities of being you identified in The Language of Values exercise earlier in this chapter. Write them down here, for easy reference.

_____

_____

_____

Read through all the instructions for this exercise before beginning. You can also listen to a guided audio recording of this exercise at http://www.newharbinger.com/54292.

Find a quiet spot where you will not be interrupted for about five minutes. Allow your eyes to gently close or find a spot in front of you to focus on with a soft gaze.

Begin by taking several long, slow, deep breaths. Breathe in fully and exhale slowly. Shift your attention from outside yourself to inside yourself, letting go of noises around you. If you are distracted by sounds in the room, simply notice this and bring your focus back to your breathing.

Imagine being in your home, during a typical day, maybe engaged in your typical activities. Call a quality of being that you value to mind and imagine what you might do or think to live it in that moment.

- *What do you observe yourself doing?*

- *Is it in addition to your usual routine? Maybe it's an activity that replaces part of your current routine.*

- *What different actions are you taking?*

- *Do any shifts in perspective guide your actions in the moment?*

- *Do you notice yourself thinking or feeling differently?*

Take a few moments to observe what is the same, along with what is different and new. Notice how these changes, additions, and shifts affect what happens in the next moments.

Do these actions lead to more new and different actions? If there are others around you, do they respond to you differently?

Take several moments to observe as much as you are able. If you are having difficulty imagining yourself doing anything new, take a few slow breaths, and extend kindness and compassion to the self that you are seeing in your mind's eye. Then try again. When you are ready, slowly open your eyes.

What did you observe about your daily routine that was new and different?

_____

_____

_____

What stayed the same in how you go about your days?

_____

_____

_____

How did you feel as you acted in new ways?

_____

_____

_____

Was your Inner Critic present? If so, what was it saying?

_____

_____

_____

Repeat this exercise for each of the qualities of action you wrote down. You can download this worksheet for reuse at http://www.newharbinger.com/54292.

If you were able to envision even one action that moves you in the direction of how you want to live your life, congratulations! You have done it! You now have an action goal. If you were not able to imagine one action goal, this would be a good time to go through the steps of CARE to notice what is getting in the way. Visit http://www.newharbinger.com/54292 to download and print the CARE worksheet, titled The Four Steps to a Self-Compassionate Voice.

Maintaining Your Goals

The biggest obstacle to "doing" values is not always identifying goals. It's sticking with the "doing" part. This is true for our own experiences and countless clients we have worked with, because even if you are able to come up with action goals, your Inner Critic might tell you to do something else. Now's the time to pay close attention to what the critical voice is saying and *closer attention* to The Coach's reminders of what's truly important.

Every year, between January 1st and February 28th, crowds of people determine to get in shape and get healthy. They flock to gyms across the world. But by the end of February, they're gone. Did they change their minds? What might cause well-intentioned people to stop taking action on health goals? For many, it's the Inner Critic telling them they can't or shouldn't follow through. This may have happened to you. It certainly has been the case for us. Let's explore your experience of this more.

Exercise: The Best-Laid Plans

Think of a time you set goals to do something important or meaningful to you but didn't follow through. Maybe you wanted to learn a new sport. To quit smoking. To curse less in front of your children. Write the original goal down.

_____

What about that goal was important to you? Write down the reasons.

_____

_____

_____

Now write down all the reasons why you ultimately did not follow through.

_____

_____

_____

Consider what you know about your Inner Critic and how it talks to you. Can you identify additional reasons why you stopped the activity? Were there critical messages like _you can't_ or _you shouldn't_ or _why bother?_ Other criticisms or fears? Write as many as you can identify.

_____

_____

_____

Try bringing compassion to your critic. For each critical or pessimistic message you were able to identify, respond with gentle and compassionate understanding. Write down those responses.

_____

_____

_____

Offer yourself alternative messages, from The Coach's perspective. List what you imagine your coach could have said that would have supported your ability to follow through.

_____

_____

_____

You may not always be able to stop the Inner Critic from telling you what you can't or shouldn't do. But you can catch that voice and offer a kinder voice instead—one that keeps you moving toward what's important. When the critical voice tries to derail you, your compassionate voice can remind you of your values. And by using benchmarks, you can keep moving toward them.

Benchmarks Keep You Going

Benchmarks can remind you that you are making progress toward meeting values-oriented goals. Say a friend invites you to their home. They tell you that they live southeast of where you live. Because it's important to see your friend (you value strong connections with others) and you know that you will have to drive to their house, you get in your car and…just start driving? Nope! Either your friend or a navigation app will offer specific directions to reach your destination. There are landmarks or cues along the way—like passing the park, turning right at the brick building, finding the neighborhood entrance—that let you know you are still on the correct route. When you question or doubt whether you are heading in the right direction, these benchmarks confirm your progress. In this way:

- values are your general direction

- goals are actions you take to move you toward what you value

- benchmarks are ways to measure your progress toward accomplishing those goals

You can use benchmarks to measure your progress toward goals every day. Let's explore benchmarks in the context of values and self-compassion through Kay's experience. Kay was strongly triggered by a photo that surfaced, evoking memories of a traumatic event. Once again, she become full of self-loathing and self-criticism. She was in a constant state of suffering and really needed to access The Coach so she could quiet her Inner Critic. Here's how she was able to recognize her values, name her goals, and identify benchmarks that helped bring compassion to her critical inner voice.

Value 1: *Having a sense of peace and well-being about myself.*

Goal: *Being around people who help me see the best in me.*

Benchmarks: *Going to a prayer circle to be validated by others for burning the photo; experiencing the prayer circle as a safe and loving environment; hearing others' stories of doing the best they can with their pain.*

Kay offers an example of how you know you are moving in a values-driven direction. With these directions laid out, when you fall off course, you can get back on. And if you ever lapse into behaviors that are contradictory to your values at the behest of your self-critic, you will be prepared to redirect and get back on track.

Exercise: Use Benchmarks to Stay On Course

Use your responses in this chapter's previous exercises to help you complete this activity. Brought together, they'll help you identify benchmarks for your values-based actions.

Choose one specific value that's important to you and reflects what you want your life to be about. Write down a value you would like to embody.

_____

What is at least one goal that will get you there? This is something that, when achieved, will express this value in your life. Write it down.

_____

_____

Now consider what you can do that will let you know you're moving in the right direction toward your goal and overarching value. Write down at least one benchmark and add more if possible.

_____

_____

_____

_____

Repeat this exercise for at least two more values. You can download this worksheet at http://www .newharbinger.com/54292 to fill out as many times as you like. Refer back to these worksheets when you are ready to take action toward more of your values and to identify new goals and benchmarks.

Our Inner Critic often pushes aside, or cautions against, doing what we value, things we hold dear, and activities that bring meaning and purpose to our lives. When we follow its warnings rather than what is in our hearts, we suffer and miss out on living a rich, full life. In this chapter, you recognized and named your personal values and explored how you can act in order to realize them. It isn't enough to identify values, they require action. Goals help you define the actions that will move you in the direction of your values. As you take steps forward, it's important to recognize what gets in the way of reaching those goals. When your Inner Critic causes doubt or confusion, having and trusting benchmarks will help you know you are on your way.

CHAPTER 7

Commit to Acting with Compassion

You are now putting one foot in front of the other. You are taking action on your values and making lasting peace with your Inner Critic in the process—even when it's likely to be loudest. There can be pain involved in moving toward what matters to you. It's likely scary to navigate life differently. As you explore life guided by The Coach rather than the Inner Critic, consider what a critical inner voice has cost you. It has cost far too much. When you begin to respond differently to what life brings, you are better able to refrain from lapses into harsh self-criticism, self-punishment, and shame. Your willingness to meet your pain with compassion can be an opportunity to live a rich and full life.

There *does not* have to be the suffering that goes along with your pain. *Pain* is the experience of mistakes, stress, failure, regret, or loss. It is part of the price of admission for being on this planet, caring for yourself, caring for others, loving, dreaming, and living a life of meaning. Pain lets you know how important your life is and how much you want to embrace the things you care about deeply.

Suffering adds to that pain by lingering on it, ruminating over stresses or mistakes or failures, and trying to avoid pain altogether. These reactions to pain only make it more conspicuous. They limit your life, which is *not* part of the price of admission. Suffering ends up holding you back, not pain.

The key to relating with pain is to continue practicing self-kindness all along the way. As you build the necessary skills for treating yourself with compassion, know that by choosing to take action, over and over again, in the service of what is important to you—even in the face of challenge and discomfort—you develop commitment to this self-compassionate way of life. The promise is in the practice.

This chapter will help you develop a commitment to self-compassion through the art of day-to-day practice. It is time for you to independently apply all the skills you have developed so far. This is an art, because the process is different from a series of sequential steps that you commit to memory and go do. Rather, you'll need resourcefulness, a trial-and-error approach, and the willingness to learn what you need to explore what works and what doesn't work. There is not a "right" thing to do "next." You likely take this trial and error, "artful" approach in other aspects of your life. For instance, you can follow the standard recipe for spaghetti sauce, but to tailor it to meet your changing taste preferences, you might play around with the amount of basil and oregano you add each time you make it. Or experiment with a different brand of canned tomatoes. Or adjust it for the number of dinner guests you are hosting.

The practice of acting with compassion includes: committing to action, recognizing that you have choices, intentionally choosing values-based actions, practicing all the time—even when the stakes don't feel high—and maintaining compassion for yourself and others. Let's take a look at each of these facets of compassionate action.

Call to Action

What does it mean to *commit* to something? Depending on the source, you might find definitions like "to pledge or promise." Yet, a promise to do something is not the same thing as doing the thing. A more accurate definition for our purposes is "to carry out or perform." This is the type of commitment we would like you to consider.

Shawn remembers learning how to scuba dive. Reading the textbook, hearing the instructor teach, taking skills quizzes, pantomiming rescue breathing with a partner, imagining what it would be like to move thirty feet below the surface. She could envision it. Think about it. Pledge to do it. But the experience of doing it (actually getting in the water, descending down, down, down, remembering to read the gauges, taking note of landmarks, taking off the mask underwater) was a completely different experience. Despite having memorized the sequence of steps and safety practices, she had to get in the water to dive—again and again and again—until she was no longer stumbling with stops and starts, until it all became fluid and routine.

It's time for you to dive. To take action. To move from reasons, intentions, feelings, and sensations to actually doing the things you want to do. You may be standing at the edge of the diving board, and you're no longer thinking about jumping—your toes are pushing off!

Exercise: Move from Thinking to Doing

Recall a time when you have been at the "end of the diving board," on the brink of taking action before. What was it like to go from thinking it to doing it? Write about what made the doing happen.

_____

_____

_____

_____

How did you feel after you did it?

_____

_____

What was the result of the action you took?

_____

_____

_____

Choosing Actions

Throughout this workbook, we have been pointing out how automatically the Inner Critic shows up to shut us down, make us feel small, and at times even powerless and hopeless. When the time comes to choose our actions, we have a choice. Here is where you get to put self-compassion into action. There is a space between the situations that activate your self-critic—and your response. As difficult as choosing may seem, at times, there is, in fact, always a choice. After initial feelings come up, the skills you have practiced so far will empower you to make a choice that moves you toward how you want to live.

Here's an example of how commitment works. A few years ago, we thought about leading a workshop on the topic of this book. While we talked about it for a long time, we didn't act on it. Consequently, no workshop happened. But then we submitted a proposal to a conference, and the workshop was accepted. We had a date. We were committed: if we didn't hold the workshop, we'd let people down, and our professional reputations might suffer. With a date on the calendar, we were committed to doing the workshop. Even though our Inner Critics were still telling us that the workshop was going to fail, we had to shift away from our fearful avoidance to begin planning next steps. With The Coach chiming in supportively, we took those steps in a constant stream of tiny actions that moved us toward our goal. Having shifted perspective after a date appeared on the calendar, we were no longer thinking. We were doing.

Exercise: You Get to Choose

Refer to the previous exercise you did. Consider the same situation in which you were able to take action.

What shifted in that moment between considering doing something and actually doing it? That is, of all the things happening inside of your skin, was there a split second when your mind told your muscles to move, push off, do the action? Describe that space.

_____

_____

_____

_____

_____

There is a Native American story about a chief sharing wisdom with his grandchild. He suggests that a great unrest exists in all humans, like two battling wolves. One wolf is possessed by painful feelings of sorrow, anger, regret, and self-pity. The other is filled with peaceful feelings of love, joy, faith, and kindness. The young grandchild asks which wolf ultimately wins the battle. The chief responds, "The one you feed."

When your Inner Critic is activated, a fight is going on inside you—between the critical voice and the self-compassionate voice. This is when you can use your observer, CARE, and values skills to help you choose. First observe what is happening. Then apply the CARE process and recall your values. This will help you choose which voice you want to lead your actions.

The following exercise may feel a bit repetitive. It is. Change happens when it becomes habitual, so the more you practice responding to the Inner Critic, the more skillful you will become at quieting it. Practice is so integral to behavior change that we invite you to repeat the following exercise several times a week, even after you finish this workbook.

Exercise: Choosing Compassion

Think of something your Inner Critic is harshly saying to you right now. Today. Describe the situation you are in that has triggered your Inner Critic.

_____

_____

_____

_____

Using your observation skills, feel the conflict inside you. Connect with what is happening, what you are thinking and feeling, and what sensations you are experiencing as a result of your Inner Critic's message.

What physical sensations are you experiencing?

_____

_____

What emotions are you experiencing?

_____

_____

What thoughts are running through your mind?

_____

_____

Now recall your values, referring to the previous chapter if needed. What ways of being, or values, matter to you about this situation?

_____

_____

What is preventing you from moving in the direction of your values?

_____

_____

_____

_____

What is your Inner Critic saying to you? Write down what you're hearing.

_____

_____

_____

_____

What is this critical voice promising to help you with? Maybe it's offering a harsh means of motivation or comparison. Perhaps it is trying to help you avoid discomfort. Describe the outcome it is promising.

_____

_____

How will that outcome help you move toward what is important and what matters? Or is it actually getting in your way? Reflect on this in writing.

_____

_____

_____

_____

Now that you have connected with your experience of the struggle between your critical voice and self-compassionate voice, it's time to practice CARE. By applying your CARE skills, you will be able to choose a path forward.

Connect with yourself. Use your breathing to maintain awareness of what is happening in your body. Keep your focus on the present moment when it begins to wander to other things.

Allow whatever thoughts, feelings, and bodily sensations you are experiencing to be present. Notice if you are struggling to get rid of, or avoid, your experience. Is the voice of the Inner Critic loud? If you are struggling to rid yourself of these experiences, continue to practice your _connecting_ and _allowing_. Make some more room for all that you are experiencing by noticing and labeling your judgments or evaluations, and then letting them be.

Respond to yourself with kindness. As you stay connected to the present moment and your internal experiences, making room for whatever is coming up, see if you are able to _respond_ to whatever is happening (thoughts, feelings, sensations) with self-compassion. Are you able to move toward your discomfort with soft, gentle kindness? Be intentional about choosing compassion.

Embrace what is happening in the moment, without judgment. Let yourself be connected to what is happening; make room for all of your thoughts, feelings, and sensations; notice when the judging voice of the Inner Critic comes up. Now, make room to recall your values and consider what action will move you toward what feels important and meaningful in this moment. What do you want to happen? If you are having trouble, use your envisioning skills to see yourself, right here and now, moving in the direction of what you value.

When you have completed CARE, write down your thoughts on how it went. What felt easy to do? What was challenging? What might you do differently next time?

_____

_____

_____

_____

_____

Looking at what worked in this exercise and what didn't will help you when a similar situation shows up in the future. This way, when it does, you can be sure you have an alternative, more effective way of behaving. Change your course of action by choosing compassion!

Taking Values-Based Actions

Change is really what this whole book is about. We're encouraging you to move away from the choices the harsh Inner Critic has you repeating and toward what you want for yourself—a life with less suffering and more meaning.

When you picked up this book, you were likely tired of feeling awful all the time. You likely were not moving in the direction of where you wanted to go. Now, through the practice of connecting with what you want your life to be about—step by step, action by action, every day—you can commit to act with self-compassion and kindness toward yourself so you can move in the direction you choose.

Holding your values close at hand every day is a helpful way to keep them in the forefront of your mind. Then, you can draw upon them to make behavioral choices. Shawn writes them down where she can see them: on sticky notes that she puts on the mirror and her desk. Come up with a way to remind yourself. Get creative. What matters to you, matters.

I will remind myself of my values by: _____

_____

Here's how Claire reminded herself of what is important. She identified kindness, nonjudgment, and creativity as some of her values.

It was easy for Claire to extend kindness and nonjudgment to other people. She had already lived much of her life focusing on the needs of the people around her, which naturally translated into acts of kindness and consideration. But Claire was still not acting very kindly toward herself. She often accepted the self-judgments that her Inner Critic was constantly offering. As long as she did this, she couldn't say she was truly practicing her values of kindness and nonjudgment.

Claire initially focused on giving herself kindness by mimicking the mini acts of kindness and thoughtfulness she extended to others. She placed a sticky note on her bathroom mirror that stated, "Do one kind thing for yourself each day." And she did. She treated herself to a decadent meal at a nice restaurant. Then went home and cooked her husband an elaborate meal out of guilt. Claire planned a "night off" for pampering with a hot bath, fuzzy robe, a bowl of ice cream, and a movie to watch from bed. She took the bath but did not stay long because she felt silly and uncomfortable (she never liked baths). She ended up not eating the ice cream because she felt badly that it wasn't on her diet plan. Then she fell asleep watching the movie because it wasn't all that interesting.

While Claire thought doing nice things for herself would feel good, she felt more distressed than ever. Her self-critic accused her of being *frivolous* and *indulgent*. Then Claire realized that while she had been acting kindly toward herself, her actions had been motivated by what she thought she should be doing, not what genuinely reflected what was important to her.

The following week, Claire put up a sticky note that read, "Do one kind thing for yourself, something that you want to do!" She again planned a pampered evening off. But once again, the Inner Critic yelled that she was *frivolous* and *indulgent*. This time, she checked the sticky note on her mirror and allowed the voice of The Coach to soften the harsh thoughts. The Coach offered: *Everyone deserves a night off, even you Claire.* Then she took her painting supplies to the park for a painting session.

Exercise: Keeping Yourself Accountable

Refer to the exercise called Your Life Domains in chapter 6 and review the values and life domains that you rated highest in importance but lowest for priority. Consider what can you do to make what matters most in your life more prominent. Here are Shawn's example responses.

One value I'd like to act upon more in my life: **Kindness.**

What goal will help me make this value a priority? **Creating connections with people I disagree with or don't understand.**

How could I start working toward that goal? What are three practical, doable baby steps that I can take this week?

1. **Exercise more patience by counting to ten before I say anything.**

2. **Remember my value of curiosity and ask at least three questions.**

3. **Include at least one kind comment in a conversation.**

What might get in the way? List thoughts, feelings, sensations, or images that might try to thwart my attempts. **Impatience, frustration, irritation, thoughts and images of being right.**

Can I make space for that stuff and take those baby steps anyway? Why or why not? **Yes. Because this is what I want to do, this is how I want to be.**

Has my Inner Critic shown up? What is it saying? **It has. It tells me that I won't be able to do it at all, much less all the time—or in the right way.**

Can I share my goals and benchmarks with a trusted friend? Who can I tell about my goals so they help me stay accountable to them? **Holly knows I am working on this. She is always there to help me walk through these steps nonjudgmentally.**

What can I say to my critic to show it compassion and settle it down?

That I understand it might feel uncomfortable to try and not always get it right, but it is important to try.

Now it's your turn.

One value I'd like to act upon more in my life: _____

What goal will help me make this value a priority? _____

_____

How can I start working toward that goal? What are three practical, doable baby steps that I can take this week?

    1. _____

    2. _____

    3. _____

What might get in the way? List thoughts, feelings, sensations, or images that might try to thwart your attempts.

_____

_____

Can I make space for that stuff and take those baby steps anyway? Why or why not?

_____

_____

Has my Inner Critic shown up? What is it saying?

_____

_____

Can I share my goals and benchmarks with a trusted friend? Who can I tell about my goals to help me stay accountable to them?

_____

_____

_____

What can I say to my critic to show it compassion and settle it down?

_____

_____

_____

_____

Committing to Your Practice

When we talk about change, we aren't simply recommending that you change for the sake of novelty. We are talking about your purpose, so that you change with intentionality. Committing to change includes reminding yourself, again and again, of the reasons you have for making change in the first place. Then, you commit to follow through because change is important and vital. Committing to change means doing the actions, whether or not your Inner Critic tries to persuade you from taking a risk, beats you up for feeling vulnerable, or ridicules you for being imperfect. Committing to change includes listening for, and heeding, the quiet and self-compassionate voice of The Coach who understands that the way you want to live—with less suffering and more fulfillment—is important to you.

Another definition of commitment is _constancy_: developing a consistently repetitive practice. This is how you can shift from talking about doing to actually doing. Becoming proficient with self-compassionate action requires more than just remembering to speak to yourself kindly when the critical voice interferes with your life in big or painful ways. Practice helps you use the skills all the time, even when the going is easy, so they become second nature—a habit.

When the going is easy, it's especially important to practice. Those are the moments when you have greater emotional resources for thinking and less interference from your Inner Critic. In times of emotional pain, when the critical voice is shouting, it may be difficult to recall the steps or techniques you need in that moment. Once the process is well practiced, however, you will be able to reach for them automatically. Consistent practice never ends if you want to keep your skills sharp. You can't learn the skills of self-compassion, use them a few times, and think, _That's it. Good to go._ To maintain the skills, you have to keep practicing them. Constantly.

Did you learn a skill as a child—maybe to play a musical instrument—and then stopped as an adult? At one time, you could probably perform that skill pretty well. Because you stopped practicing at some point, how would you do now? Would you be rusty? Fumbling around to get it right? On the other hand, perhaps there is a skill that you learned when young that you have continued to use. Are you as good now as then? Better? You are probably familiar with the saying "use it or lose it." As we have shared before, the promise is in the practice.

Exercise: Practice, Practice, Practice

Write down seven acts of self-compassion that you can practice this week, one for each day of the week. Commit to doing them at least twice each day.

Monday: _____

Tuesday: _____

Wednesday: _____

Thursday: _____

Friday: _____

Saturday: _____

Sunday: _____

What was it like to practice self-compassion every day for a week? Did any of the skills or actions come more easily to you?

_____

_____

_____

_____

_____

Are you more likely to practice consistently if you write down your actions? Set reminders for yourself? What else will help you to get into an ongoing, consistent *practice*?

_____

_____

_____

_____

As you commit to your practice, be sure to ask yourself, *What will happen if I don't commit to* _____? *How will I feel? What will I think of myself?* The answers to those questions are called *consequences*. Consequences drive behavior.

Consider these answers to those questions: *I will feel ashamed of myself if I don't take this exam.* Or, *I will feel lonely if I don't accept this invitation.* The consequence of shame and loneliness can inform you when choosing a more effective behavior in the future.

To be clear, looking at consequences is not about punishing yourself. It is the opposite, really. When we were just talking and thinking about creating a workshop on this topic, all the thinking and talking actually led to *not* doing anything. Only when facing the potential consequence of not holding the workshop once the submission was accepted, could we reconnect with what was important and do the activities required. A couple of feelings and thoughts were: *We wouldn't reach the people we know we could help. We would feel so disappointed in ourselves by giving in to our fear of rejection.* The consequences of not acting were the very things that encouraged us to act.

A focus on consequences should remain values-driven, not punitive or self-critical. That is, make sure you recognize consequences because they reflect your pursuit or neglect of a value that's meaningful to you. It's not because they reflect your Inner Critic's harsh expectation or unrealistic self-concept.

Bring to mind a current goal you're struggling to take values-based action toward. Review the steps you need to take and notice which steps are bringing about an urge to avoid it. Note what actions are causing your critic to say, *No, you don't need to do that right now.* Pause for a moment, then write down the consequences—informed by your values—that could happen if you *don't* take this step.

_____

_____

_____

_____

Common Humanity and Compassion for All

Many things bind us together as human beings. We are all imperfect. We all have a need for connection. We all suffer at one time or another. When we can recognize our universal experiences, without comparing our pain as better or worse than anyone else's, we have an opportunity to truly connect with one another and ourselves. In chapter 4, we identified common humanity as one of the three components of compassion (Germer and Neff 2013). Here, we are offering you the concept of common humanity as a way to choose to take action toward your goals.

You may be very good at offering compassion to others. When you are able to recognize that you are also deserving of the compassion you extend to others, you can direct the very same to yourself. With this exercise, you will be on your way to practicing self-compassion in a way that infuses action.

Exercise: Meeting Yourself with Compassion

Bring to mind something important to you that you want to take action around. Consider a painful or challenging situation, thought, or feeling, and write it down. It could be the very same goal you identified in the previous exercise, a new goal, or a baby step toward living a value.

_____

_____

_____

As you did in the previous exercise, identify the obstacles that get in the way of doing what matters.

_____

_____

_____

Imagine that someone you care about is telling you about the painful situation, the thing they want to do, and the obstacles that get in the way. Write down how you would offer compassion to them. What would you say and how would you act toward them?

_____

_____

_____

_____

Now, picture them having the same pain that you are having, the same struggles, maybe the same suffering. Let yourself remember that you are that person wanting the same compassionate voice. Write what you can say to yourself.

_____

_____

_____

_____

_____

Common humanity lets you know that you are not alone on this journey. It lets you know that you, as a human being, have a right to kindness and grace. People find healing in another's compassionate presence. You can find that same healing when you extend it to yourself too.

This is not a one-and-done deal, though. We ask that you practice and then keep practicing. Bring that common sense of humanity to all areas of your life: those that are working well and those that are not. Keep a journal handy so you can gain consistency in this practice. Write down every time you see a chance to shower yourself with compassion. That is the consistency, the practice. When you find yourself feeling that you are the only one who is struggling, remember you are not alone.

Commitment to compassionate action moves you from promises to a life of intentional acts. When you commit to making intentional choices whenever possible, you free yourself to choose to act in the direction of what is important. Commitment to intentional action also involves consistent and frequent practice, especially at times when the stakes are low, so that you are prepared and less likely to falter when the situation is emotionally charged. When you let yourself open up to common humanity, you can offer yourself the same compassion and gentle kindness that you bestow upon others. Common humanity also fosters a sense of connection, belonging, and worth. Using all the skills in your toolbox, you can commit to choosing action aimed toward the realization of your values, which will bring your life meaning.

CHAPTER 8

Troubleshooting for When Compassion Doesn't Come Easily

Hopefully you now have a sense of what you can do to quiet your Inner Critic. You have gradually put together all the skills introduced in each chapter and practiced them with every page turned. You're familiar with how to observe your experience, identify the voice of the critic, acknowledge the contexts in which it came into existence, respond with CARE, connect with your values, make behavioral choices, and commit to practicing with consistency. And for each and every step, you are prepared to bring a gentle sense of kindness and self-compassion.

Now that you have read this book, we'd like to say that you're good to go. Roger, over and out. Alas, it's not so simple. Another thing about human nature, which you might know about yourself, is that adding new behaviors and getting into a routine with them is difficult. We get into grooves, and it is hard to expand beyond those old habits. Bringing compassion to yourself in order to quiet the harsh inner voice is challenging work. Undoubtedly, at some point, you may find yourself struggling to use the skills you have practiced. In this chapter, we'll explore how to address the obstacles that may come up as you choose compassion and values-driven action. Through the course of our own personal work addressing our Inner Critics, as well as our work with numerous clients, we have found that people struggle most to stay the course with self-compassion when the following obstacles show up.

- avoidance

- truthful-sounding stories and hard-and-fast rules

- conflicting values-guided actions

- major life events and big emotions

- lack of support from others

- struggling to remember what to do

Avoidance

Avoidance happens because your Inner Critic exists to guide you away from discomfort, whatever the cost. And we know that running away from unpleasant emotions often means moving away from the very things that matter. It may cost us meaning, purpose, and vitality. We cannot emphasize this enough.

To address avoidance, you must be on the lookout for it. Developing a consistent practice of your CARE observation skills will help you familiarize yourself with what your avoidance looks like. As you build a daily habit of self-observation, you may come to recognize patterns of avoidance. These can include: the specific things your Inner Critic tells you when it is encouraging you to avoid, the sensations you feel in your body with avoidance, and the types of challenges and situations your Inner Critic most often encourages you to avoid. When avoidance does show up, in addition to your CARE practice, we recommend:

- journaling about your experiences in order to gain perspective

- looking at the consequences of your avoidant behavior by asking yourself, *What will it cost me?*

- envisioning yourself doing the thing that matters

- listening to The Coach, the voice that will guide you away from avoidance and into action

- practicing exercises that have been most helpful to you while moving through this workbook

Truthful-Sounding Stories

Some stories are so compelling, they must be true. But these narratives can be tricky. Ask yourself, *Does the story I'm telling myself keep me stuck, or is it moving toward what is important?* Remember, when you meet yourself with compassion, you can transform your history into the stories that drive you forward. When you identify your values—what you want your life to be about—that is where your new story can begin. Yes, you want to honor your history as an important part of your experience. Yet when you realize that these stories no longer serve you, there is a chance to write your story from now on.

Exercise: Your Story 2.0

Write the history that was; the one that no longer fits.

_____

_____

_____

_____

_____

_____

_____

_____

_____

_____

_____

Now write the story that is or that you want to live. Think big—this is your story!

_____

_____

_____

_____

_____

_____

_____

_____

_____

_____

Conflicting Values

Sometimes you may run into trouble when your values lead you in different directions and result in competing demands. You may have to choose between a work emergency or seeing your child in a playoff game. Other values conflicts may cause more pain, like choosing between leaving an unfulfilling marriage or keeping a family intact. At times, you may have to choose from among things so important they feel as if they're woven into the fabric of who you are.

Here's the bottom line: When both choices reflect important values, choosing may be difficult, and yet you won't choose wrong. This is where meeting yourself with self-compassion comes into play. Self-compassion helps you navigate complicated and even painful decisions with far less suffering.

Exercise: Bringing Compassion to the Conflict

Write about a time when you had to choose between two things that mattered to you.

_____

_____

_____

What did you say to yourself?

_____

_____

_____

If you met yourself with compassion then, bravo! If not, what can you say kindly to yourself now?

_____

_____

_____

_____

Major Life Events and Big Emotions

When big things happen, big emotions happen. The Inner Critic kicks in automatically. Your work here is to treat yourself with compassion as you remember common humanity. Your big life events come with big emotions because they are indications that you value the thing that has caused them to come to the surface in the first place. Whether it's a loss, missed opportunity, heartache—whatever the circumstance—you know that it is wrapped in what you value.

The critical voice will jump right in here, telling you: _You didn't do enough, You did something wrong, You shoulda, coulda, woulda_ whatever. By now you know that bringing compassion to these big emotions and life events will ease that critical voice and soften the blow. Self-compassion will remind you that you are struggling with things that matter to you and that those values deserve the big emotions. Let's repeat the previous exercise with big emotions in mind.

Exercise: Big Events

Bring to mind an important life event that may have come with a big emotion. Write about how you experienced it.

What was the major life event and what was the big emotion that accompanied it?

_____

_____

_____

_____

How did you experience it?

_____

_____

What did you feel?

_____

_____

How did you act?

_____

_____

What did you think about how you showed up and acted?

_____

_____

_____

_____

If you met yourself with compassion, bravo! If you didn't, how could you offer yourself compassion now?

_____

_____

_____

_____

Big emotions and life events are going to happen, as long as we are alive. By identifying how you would like to offer yourself compassion during those times, you have the opportunity to do something different when they show up next.

Lack of Support

It's challenging enough doing this work. What happens when you don't have a safe person to lean on? In chapter 5, we discussed connecting with others. The support of loved ones is vital when you are struggling. Our society, particularly our media, reinforces the Inner Critic's voice and pushes you to buy into the scripts that move you away from your own authentic values. This is when you need to reach out to a friend, trusted group or association, community resource, or mentor—because you need a great coach when your own coach is being bullied by the critic.

Struggling to Remember What to Do

In elementary schools, fire drills are a regular practice. We grow up knowing how to handle this emergency—not just intellectually, but with sirens blasting, we can calmly move out of buildings and stand quietly while someone in charge calls names to make sure everyone is accounted for. As our bodies practice, should a fire ever rage, the hope is that muscle memory will kick in. The same is true when it comes to self-compassion. If you have a regular practice, self-compassion will come readily. This is what you want when the stakes seem really high, when you feel overwhelmed and dysregulated. If you stop practicing, you'll likely revert back to old, familiar, unhelpful coping strategies.

It's wise to practice self-compassion when you are not emotionally elevated so that you have the skill to call on when rough times come front and center. It's the same as practicing a fire drill. To extend compassion to yourself in times of relative well-being, you will be equally prepared to do so during times of strife, so you can move through those painful experiences with skill. Yes, you may have tears, but you will meet those tears with loving-kindness automatically.

Our resources for troubleshooting are not an exhaustive list. In fact, you may be your greatest resource of all. If you have begun the practice of extending kindness and compassion to yourself, you may be beginning to recognize that you have so much to give to yourself.

What Gifts Do You Have to Give Yourself?

Get creative and extend compassion to yourself in ways that are unique to you. For example, if you are spiritual or religious, we invite you to embrace the practices from those traditions that help you find and receive self-compassion. Or maybe you find self-compassion through art. Or nature. Many people find unique gateways to self-compassion. Whatever gifts you have that bring a sense of mastery, skill, and light to what you value, use them to foster tenderness and loving-kindness in a way that creates worthiness and belonging.

Exercise: The Gifts You Give Yourself

What are some of your spiritual practices, such as meditation, prayer, or other rituals?

_____

_____

_____

_____

How have those practices invited self-compassion?

_____

_____

If you have found self-compassion through having compassion for others, embrace those practices. Maybe it's through service to your community or volunteering in some way. If you have found self-compassion through having compassion for others, write about it. How have you extended compassion to others?

_____

_____

_____

_____

How has that helped you extend compassion to yourself?

_____

_____

_____

So often when your Inner Critic takes over, you can forget what is working or has worked in your life. Identify situations in which you feel masterful and skillful. Perhaps it is in a hobby. Maybe it's in the way you treat and care for people you love.

Where: Write down where you feel a sense of mastery or skill. For example: *I feel masterful and skillful at work.*

_____

_____

_____

_____

How: Identify how this shows up. For example: *I feel skillful when I appear confident in a meeting, look people in the eye, stand up, and engage people during presentations.*

_____

_____

_____

_____

Remembering to recognize the skills and gifts you have to give yourself is another form of self-compassion.

After working through his book, you know how your critical inner voice came to be. You know what it costs you. You know how to slow down, to observe, and to CARE. You have been able to identify what's really important to you and recognize behaviors that get in the way. We have walked you through how to commit to this practice of self-compassion. Knowing all that you now know about yourself, we encourage you to invite yourself to this way of living.

Exercise: Letter to Me

In the space that follows, write a letter to you, inviting yourself to practice self-compassion. Here's an example.

> Dear One,
>
> I am scared and I know this is hard. I know the voice of the Inner Critic has cost me more than I am now willing to pay. I don't want the fear to stop me anymore. I don't want the "I am not good enough" messages to get in the way anymore. I have let this stop me long enough. I now commit to moving forward, toward the things that make me feel worthy and fulfilled. I commit to offering myself mindful intention. To opening up to what I want my life to be about.
>
> With love to me,
>
> Me

Write a letter to yourself.

_____

_____

_____

_____

_____

_____

_____

_____

When you feel yourself moving away from what matters, let this letter of love be a reminder to come back to self-compassion and quiet your Inner Critic.

Living a rich, full life is simultaneously rewarding and challenging. Obstacles to the practice of self-compassion and quieting your Inner Critic are likely to show up. Even after you are well-versed in the practice of self-compassion, you may struggle with choosing what to do. By slowing down and practicing self-compassion, in all the forms found in this workbook, you can move through those struggles. You can return to acting in directions that lead to meaning, purpose, and vitality. Tap into your own creativity and resourcefulness as gifts and additional gateways to self-compassion.

Dear Readers

As we thought about how to wrap up this workbook, we each reflected on what it has been like to share our personal experiences and vulnerability with you. Sharing vulnerability with each other has been a gift over the years and we have realized that doing so with you, too, is another gift for us.

We shared how we put our values into action when creating this workbook. The process began with a friendship borne out of an ache for genuine connection, unlike many of our previous friendships. Together, realizing vulnerability and gentle nonjudgment not only felt like a safe experience, it was also empowering. We met each other at a time when we both felt small and not enough. We were willing to see, and be seen by, one another. Through that, we found a compassionate connection. We became each other's safe space at a time when we didn't think it was possible. Within each other's safety, we were able to practice self-compassion.

It hasn't always been easy. Being vulnerable and genuine with another is scary and often uncomfortable. We share this with you because we have walked this walk and continue to walk it. We flexed every single one of our self-compassion skills and common humanity while writing this workbook. There were many times we didn't think we could or should—and we did. We want you to know that you can move toward important values too. We encourage you to do the thing that makes your heart sing and soul dance.

With love and compassion,

Holly and Shawn

References

Bandura, A., and R. H. Walters. 1977. *Social Learning Theory. Vol. 1.* Englewood Cliffs, NJ: Prentice-Hall.

Bowlby, J. 1969. *Attachment. Attachment and Loss: Vol. 1.* New York: Basic Books.

Brown, B. 2010. *The Gifts of Imperfection: Let Go of Who You Think You're Supposed to Be and Embrace Who You Are.* Center City, MN: Hazelden.

———. 2021. *Atlas of the Heart: Mapping Meaningful Connection and the Language of Human Experience.* New York: Random House.

Cannon, W. B. 1915. *Bodily Changes in Pain, Hunger, Fear, and Rage: An Account of Recent Researches into the Function of Emotional Excitement.* New York: D. Appleton & Company.

D'Argembeau, A., D. Stawarczyk, S. Majerus, F. Collette, M. Van der Linden, D. Feyers, et al. 2010. "The Neural Basis of Personal Goal Processing When Envisioning Future Events." *Journal of Cognitive Neuroscience* 22: 1701–1713.

Deutsch, M., and H. B. Gerard. 1955. "A Study of Normative and Informational Social Influences upon Individual Judgment." *The Journal of Abnormal and Social Psychology* 51: 629–636.

Festinger, L. 1954. "A Theory of Social Comparison Processes." *Human Relations* 7: 117–140.

Germer, C., and K. Neff. 2013. "Self-Compassion in Clinical Practice." *Journal of Clinical Psychology: In Session* 69: 1–12.

Gilbert, P., and J. Miles. 2000. "Sensitivity to Social Put-Down: Its Relationship to Perceptions of Social Rank, Shame, Social Anxiety, Depression, Anger and Self-Other Blame." *Personality and Individual Differences* 29: 757–774.

Gooding, D. C. 2004. "Envisioning Explanations—the Art in Science." *Interdisciplinary Science Reviews* 29: 278–294.

Hayes, S. C., D. Barnes-Holmes, and B. Roche. 2001. *Relational Frame Theory: A Post-Skinnerian Account of Human Language and Cognition*. New York: Kluwer/Plenum.

Kabat-Zinn, J. 1994. *Wherever You Go, There You Are: Mindfulness Meditation in Everyday Life*. New York: Hyperion.

Löw, C. A., H. Schauenburg, and U. Dinger. 2020. "Self-Criticism and Psychotherapy Outcome: A Systematic Review and Meta-analysis." *Clinical Psychology Review* 75: 101808.

Morgan, T. J., and K. N. Laland. 2012. "The Biological Bases of Conformity." *Frontiers in Neuroscience* 6: 87.

Naragon-Gainey, K., and D. Watson. 2012. "Personality, Structure." In *Encyclopedia of Human Behavior*, 2nd ed., edited by V. S. Ramachandran, 90–95. London: Elsevier.

Newall, N. E., J. G. Chipperfield, L. M. Daniels, S. Hladkyj, and R. P. Perry. 2009. "Regret in Later Life: Exploring Relationships Between Regret Frequency, Secondary Interpretive Control Beliefs, and Health in Older Individuals." *International Journal of Aging and Human Development* 68: 261–88.

Shahar, B., E. R. Carlin, D. E. Engle, J. Hegde, O. Szepsenwol, and H. Arkowitz. 2011. "A Pilot Investigation of Emotion-Focused Two-Chair Dialogue Intervention for Self-Criticism." *Clinical Psychology and Psychotherapy* 19: 496–507.

Sheldon, K., and S. Lyubomirsky. 2006. "How to Increase and Sustain Positive Emotion: The Effects of Expressing Gratitude and Visualizing Best Possible Selves." *The Journal of Positive Psychology* 1: 73–82.

Skinner, B. F. 1938. *The Behavior of Organisms: An Experimental Analysis*. New York: Appleton-Century-Crofts.

Walker, P. 2013. *Complex PTSD: From Surviving to Thriving: A Guide and Map for Recovering from Childhood Trauma*. Lafayette, CA: Azure Coyote.

Wills, T. A. 1981. "Downward Comparison Principles in Social Psychology." *Psychological Bulletin* 90: 245–271.

Shawn Costello Whooley, PsyD, is a psychologist, behavior change coach, and peer-reviewed acceptance and commitment therapy (ACT) trainer in private practice in Baltimore, MD. She also serves as a staff psychologist in the Trauma Recovery Program at the Baltimore VA Medical Center. Costello Whooley specializes in the use of evidence-based treatments for anxiety, trauma, and interpersonal relationship problems. She is also founder of Stillpoint Journeys, a coaching and training practice focused on moving the work of behavior change out of the office and into life by using extended hiking, horseback riding, and sailing treks to experience the processes of ACT in real time. Shawn provides ACT and contextual behavioral science (CBS) training internationally and in academic settings.

Holly Yates, MS, LCMHC, has been in private practice in North Carolina since 2004. She is trained in functional analytic psychotherapy (FAP), ACT, and dialectical behavior therapy (DBT). She is a founding facilitator of the online ACT Peer Intervision Group sponsored through the Association of Contextual Behavioral Science (ACBS), and a Certified FAP Trainer through the University of Washington. Yates has been a presenter of FAP and ACT at ACBS World Conferences since 2016, and continues to train both internationally and domestically. Yates was a plenary speaker at the ACBS Brazil Conference in 2021. She has coauthored a chapter on FAP and couples counseling which will be released in Argentina at the upcoming ACBS World Conference. Yates is on the board of ACL Global Project, and is a member of the Functional Analytic Psychotherapy International Board for Certification (FAP/CEP).

Foreword writer **Mavis Tsai, PhD,** is a clinical psychologist and senior research scientist at the University of Washington Center for Science of Social Connection. She is cofounder of FAP.

Real change *is* possible

For more than fifty years, New Harbinger has published proven-effective self-help books and pioneering workbooks to help readers of all ages and backgrounds improve mental health and well-being, and achieve lasting personal growth. In addition, our spirituality books offer profound guidance for deepening awareness and cultivating healing, self-discovery, and fulfillment.

Founded by psychologist Matthew McKay and Patrick Fanning, New Harbinger is proud to be an independent, employee-owned company. Our books reflect our core values of integrity, innovation, commitment, sustainability, compassion, and trust. Written by leaders in the field and recommended by therapists worldwide, New Harbinger books are practical, accessible, and provide real tools for real change.

 **newharbinger**publications

MORE BOOKS from
NEW HARBINGER PUBLICATIONS

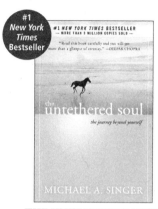

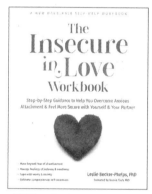

Did you know there are **free tools** you can download for this book?

Free tools are things like **worksheets**, **guided meditation exercises**, and **more** that will help you get the most out of your book.

You can download free tools for this book—whether you bought or borrowed it, in any format, from any source—from the New Harbinger website. All you need is a NewHarbinger.com account. Just use the URL provided in this book to view the free tools that are available for it. Then, click on the "download" button for the free tool you want, and follow the prompts that appear to log in to your NewHarbinger.com account and download the material.

You can also save the free tools for this book to your **Free Tools Library** so you can access them again anytime, just by logging in to your account! Just look for this button on the book's free tools page. ➤

+ Save this to my free tools library